A CONVERSATION ABOUT THE PEDAGOGICAL AND SPIRITUAL IMPACT ON TEENAGERS

Dr. Elena Lyubenova

2023

Please visit my blog:

https://phdelenalyubenova.blogspot.com/

CONTENTS

INTRODUCTION

The concept behind the present book

This book aims to discuss the pedagogical and spiritual impact that adults can have on teenagers and is written through the prism and perspective of spiritual development. In order to instil love, compassion, and care for other human beings, it is imperative that a child's spirituality is developed, irrespective of their nationality and religious affiliation.

There is often a stereotype attached to teenagers, in that their moods tend to fluctuate. Teenagers may present as happy and elated when things are seemingly going their way, however if refused a request, their mood may become hostile and unhappy. The question then lingers as to why this may be happening and as adults, what we could do to positively influence teenagers and facilitate their spiritual growth, without losing our connection with them. If one is equipped with knowledge around a teenager's emotional and physical development, then adequate methods of communication can be identified to support them. Some of which is reflected throughout this book.

It may be extremely difficult in juggling the energy, emotions and situations which arise as a parent or caregiver of a teenager, and at times you may feel as though you just want to escape this reality. It is at times like this, so we should compare ourselves with the teachers who are managing such behaviours in a classroom full of teenagers. Arguably, they are absolute heroes when it comes to the mental toughness, as they show to absorb the energy of thirty teenagers in a room every day.

The ultimate goal of upbringing and education is to raise free individuals who realise the limitations of the material world they are in and quite consciously submit their lives to the development of all the natural, intellectual, and emotional riches laid down by vast cosmic intelligence. Pieces of which are all living things on planet earth. If upbringing and education take place simultaneously with consideration of the individual characteristics of each child and are handled with respect, delicacy and understanding, then the child will develop in their own unique way. Furthermore, they will possess the abilities and desire to fly free and bold like birds, metaphorically speaking. However, if adults neglect to take into account individual characteristics, dismiss the delicate and respectful approach, with methods which are grossly authoritarian, dogmatic, over-controlling and without considering the wishes of the child, then the adult responsible may raise an individual quite the contrary. Metaphorically speaking, a bird, who is fearful with folded wings, is bound tightly to the ground. It is almost as though they are being tied by the adults who are afraid of losing the bird and therefore keep it in a cage.

As the world around us continues to evolve and develop, adults must constantly update their methods of communicating and influencing children and adolescents if they are to be adequate and adaptable to the new changing times that we are currently in. It is an era where children are more aware in every way than we have ever been. Adults must have the courage and honesty to admit to themselves that sometimes their methods of interaction and influence are not adequate and acceptable and can in turn provoke them to look for new techniques. For the sake of their children, it is worth trying and not stopping to educate ourselves and change in order to find a common language and path.

Overcoming the material limitations in which we live leads to the understanding that the spiritual dimensions are infinite and limited only by our desire to be a part of them. Realising that accumulating spiritual riches, not only makes our lives immortal, but also brings light to those around us at a time when they may be blinded by the pain of the spiritual darkness. This is a radical realisation. It is an almost revolutionary awareness, after which spreading light becomes something of a mission and a primary joy, through which we can experience life as a series of infinite possibilities. Both the upbringing and the educational process are the perfect place to ignite the spark to spiritual flight that will inspire children, who are budding teenagers, to fly with wings, with confidence strengthened by spiritual joys. This is something we, as adults, can teach children.

Parallels to my previous book, 'How to Raise A Hero'

With similar tones and themes, the current book is a continuation of 'How to Raise A Hero', with focus moving away from young children, to teenagers solely. 'How To Raise A Hero' was centred around the personality of a child, whereby the adult in their life was deemed a hero. One, who would know how to help the child develop their potential and begin to view themselves as a hero. In order for this to be the case, a combination of spiritual, intellectual, and emotional development, would benefit not only the children, but those around them. Previously, we explored the application of non-authoritarian methods and how to cultivate character traits. The main method utilised in the previous book was our love for children. Unconditional acceptance of children and adolescents as they are in view of their personality specifics, and not as we would like to see them, is essential for building healthy relationships between children and adults. Some of the ideas in this book will correspond with the ideas of the previous book.

The subject of the book

Every adult to exist would have been a teenager who was trying to grasp the developmental processes independently, as nature was pushing them forward and they were following suit. Therefore, it is imperative for adults to remember the difficulties associated with being an adolescent, and thus to know the processes children forming into adolescents are going through. Adults should take time to consciously try to build bridges with children or teenagers, not tear them down. If adults are not educated on these processes and their universal nature, which unites us with every living being on the planet or the vast Cosmos, then we run the risk of adults negatively influencing teenagers.

The purpose of 'A Conversation About The Pedagogical and Spiritual Impact on Teenagers'

The purpose of the book is to remind adults about the main developmental processes that our children and adolescents go through, so that we, as adults, can more adequately, intelligently, and modernly communicate and influence them. Let us not forget that these processes are common to humans, animals, and plants alike, which are considered living forms on the planet. Undeniably, humans stand out with greater intelligence, specifically how this intelligence is utilised. Unfortunately, there are times where adults do not use this immense intelligence that we possess as a species to improve communication with one another, to develop love, peace, and progress. All too often we knowingly use this intelligence as a tool to suppress, destroy, hate, and hold back the development of our own children.

It is crucial to recognise that children do not belong to us, rather they are given temporarily to us to be cared for. This realisation can lead to an understanding of the enormous role and responsibility we have in their lives. We, as adults, have the power to inspire children to fly, or to make them feel as though they have broken wings. In layman's terms, adults who neglect to inspire their children may instil feelings of poor self-worth and limitations on their dreams. Therefore, the responsibility of what tomorrow's generations will become, lies with the adults who are responsible for them. Techniques such as 'excessive control' is one of the fastest methods in destroying the foundation between an adult and child. This signals to the child that their parent or caregiver does not have the time and desire to hear or understand them.

Therefore, as adults, we must be knowledgeable about the specifics of the transition age and what processes children go through when becoming adolescents. It is important to remember that these developmental processes are not chosen by children to anger us and make our lives more difficult, but the vast, divine cosmic intelligence itself has chosen certain developmental processes for every living and non-living form in the entire cosmos. At least such are our scientific and non-scientific suspicions about how the cosmic energy structure develops and about the very small, almost invisible place that every human being has in it. We are a part of it. Every individual, whether it be a child, adolescent, or adult, is a part of this divine cosmic energy intelligence. In this structure, one has no gender, age and profession, as we co-exist as an energy that we can model in the form of human qualities such as character, intelligence and skills, which is individual to everyone. Each of us is a small but important part of the huge cosmic energy puzzle.

On energy level, we are similar to 'joined vessels'. Do you imagine that only happy, peaceful, joyful, harmonious vibrations take off from our planet Earth and merge with the vast Cosmos? Surely, it does not hurt to dream and attempt to then implement this in the process of upbringing and education, right? When we are informed as adults, we can also help when necessary to avoid the sometimes tragic development of situations. It is worth mentioning that when children are transitioning into adolescence, they may encounter new feelings which they find difficult to process. If an adult is unavailable for them emotionally, they may develop mental health related problems, which sadly result in the ever-growing suicide rate, which is disturbingly high amongst teenagers. Therefore, it is imperative for an adult to be emotionally available, and not absent in their teenager's world.

Structure

Later on in the book, we explore the problems adolescents may face day to day, their strengths, and weaknesses, with all the caveats of generalisations, in an emotionally accepting way. As mentioned previously, the current book possesses themes which encourage adults to learn and understand how to manage the energy of teenagers, with delicate, respectful, calm, and wise manner. In opposition to excessive over-control and authoritarianism. There is also encouragement to perceive teenagers as equals, utilising respectful dialogue, bargaining and compromises. Some of the oppositions we consider are - *"natural form - social form/structure", "nature - socialisation", "authoritarianism - humane* treatment", "flight - crawling", "biological development - spiritual development", "conscious choice - unconscious choice", "materialism - spirituality", "result - process", "knowledge - awareness", "energy inclusion - energy exclusion", "identity limitation - identity expansion", "freedom - unfreedom", "negotiation - imposition" , "upbringing - training", "dominance - dependence", "expansion - contraction", "growth - decline", "mind - heart", "passivity - activity", "biological defence mechanisms - spiritual defence mechanisms", "harmony - chaos", "pain - joy", "horizon - lack of horizon", "engagement - non-engagement".   Some of the opposition can completely separate children and adults if we do not learn to listen   to each other sensibly, delicately, intelligently, and respectfully. Yet, understanding and overcoming these same oppositions can serve as a bridge to the dialogue which will bring oppositions into unison. The choice that the child makes is also important, but additionally so is the receiving response and reaction of the adult., which can influence a child or adolescent's decision.

The Characters

Needless to say, the characters deriving in this book are the adolescent children aged 13-19 years with all the complex contradictory trends of growth and transition, as they grow older. This is an extremely sensitive and delicate age that can forever leave a lasting impression on the memories, habits, psyche, and personality of children. Moreover, this is an age where your child is not quite a child any longer and neither have, they formed quite into an adult yet. The developing human in your world begins to show interest in all things external to their daily route of family and school, seeking their place in this world and within social structures. They may exercise their voice to express an opinion, to be heard, or to make a change. The budding adolescent may show interest in how their body is changing, trying to understand the changes and that of the opposite sex. They may pay greater attention towards their looks, and how others perceive them. It is a cocktail of hormones that creates emotions that sometimes contradict each other, pulling the child in different directions.

This is an age when personal transformations are occurring, and so are the energy levels. One begins to discover their own individuality and character. This happens in order to achieve independence from the world of adults, as nature prepares them for an independent life, as it happens with the young of birds and animals. Humans are arguably the only living being on the planet in whom this stage of preparation for an independent life from the adult world lasts so long. We are effectively becoming more and more dependent on technology and many other survival mechanisms, and we are becoming more and more unable to survive on our own in a non-social environment, as in comparison with animals and birds for example. This process of natural separation from the nest in order to learn to fly and cope independently is sometimes quite deliberately hindered by adults, who may even try to stop the growing process. Let us compare with animals for a moment. Can you imagine a pigeon trying to get their baby back to their nest when they are hopping clumsily trying to learn how to fly? Can you imagine that the pigeon constantly criticizes and even abuses the little pigeon, which results in incorrect attempts to fly? In this regard, the survival instincts of animals and birds are wise. Something that we have lost in the process of surrounding ourselves as consumers with matter, which has given rise to thousands of survival mechanisms that we depend on.

Biological and spiritual evolution in humans continues. It is up to adults to support these impulses or stifle them, but they will suffer the consequences. Adults have a crucial role to play here, in that they have to recognize that total control methods are ineffective and if they want to maintain a relationship with children, they have to behave respectfully. Adolescents are no longer children, and they regard everything with adoration, faith, respect, and reverence, trusting their parents wholly. They can be highly critical and full of doubt and distrust of the norms and rules and may attempt to change them to create their own. They begin to look for themselves socially and external to the family, at times rebelling against any restrictions, as they do not like the norms and dogmas imposed on them by others. They want to participate in creating the rules of the social game. This is their way of learning independence and initiative. The transition from child to an adolescent teenager can be a very interesting, delicate, fruitful, and constructive age if adults understand the peculiarities of the processes their children are going through. Particularly if they direct energy wisely for constructive purposes, and not destructive, such as destroying their relationships. At the same time, adolescents are aware that socially they do not have the same experience as adults and hold on to them. The excessive control and criticism if perceived and experienced from an adult, can suffocate them, and break their attempts at an independent flight. This contradiction confuses and saddens them. They follow the aspirations, urges and impulses that nature has put into them, and which are common to every living organism on the planet and the vast Cosmos.

The problems come from nature pushing them in one direction and into social structures through adults pushing them in another direction. But both should not be mutually exclusive, rather complementary and compromising, in order to obtain socialisation painlessly and with consideration of the individual characteristics of children. In order to nurture and develop the cosmic intelligence, a piece of which we all appear to have, it is important pedagogically that adults understand these universal cosmic processes and aspirations, so that there are less conflict situations, and greater mutual respect, trust, and love.

The other characters of the book are the grown children, the parents, and the teachers. Adults can have different roles in the lives of adolescents, but we will refer to those adults who are in the closest environment and whose influence is strongest in a positive and negative sense. It is important not to forget that suicides in this age group are statistically on the rise. They are caused by the feeling of isolation, misunderstanding, loneliness, constant instillation of guilt and lack of way out due to tender age and lack of social experience. Adolescents must be treated with a view to their future potential spiritual status and guided along this path delicately and understandingly. We must remember that we are communicating with their soul, thoughts, and emotions.

Who is this book for?

It is for any adult, whether a parent, a caregiver, or a teacher, who bears direct influence and close contact with adolescents. It provides an occasion to think about which approach, as adults, we adopt, whether it be inertly, authoritatively, or consciously, to choose an individual approach that follows the specifics of each child.

As adults, do we listen to them and show interest, or do we just yell and use our role authority to remove communication with them, as they are seemingly interfering with our personal lives as adults? Do we choose to develop and influence them in a positive direction and thus attract them, or do we push them away with our commands, our criticisms, and our negativity? Arguably, a child or adolescent will view their own development differently and will reach their own understanding and awareness of themselves. As an adolescent growing up, they may perceive themselves with a sense of pride and self-respect, therefore earlier methods of punishment and consideration of choices, which were effective when the child was young may no longer be effective. For instance, we may manage to get a two-year-old child to go to the corner and think about their misbehaviour and reflect, however it is a greater challenge to get an adolescent to follow suit on the same punishment. As close contact adults, we should perceive them with a level of respect and alter the methods of interaction, which we were valid in their childhood years. In this sense, the book is addressed to adults in general, may it be parents, caregivers, teachers, friends, neighbours, or relatives of the teenager.

The tone of 'A Conversation About The Pedagogical and Spiritual Impact on Teenagers'

As mentioned previously, the tone and style of 'A Conversation About the Pedagogical and Spiritual Impact on Teenagers' will reflect similarities to that of 'How To Raise A Hero'. Adults full of love, respect, care, patience, and understanding can raise children full of love, respect, care, patience and understanding. The personal example and personality of the adult is of leading importance for us in the process of pedagogical upbringing, education, and impact. To this end, adults must be ready to constantly change and develop, following the specifics of each individual situation and problem. Our refusal to change and understand every problematic situation our child finds themselves in can lead to critical consequences. This is because adults are considered as the leaders. It is mandatory that the pedagogical impact is based on the absence of violence towards the child's personality.

Methodology

We combine an array of methods, inclusive of the prominent methods of painting with positive words, mirror reflection, the individual method, and the method of conscious concentrated attention. A willingness to spend time and attention, and to listen is also essential.

What content will not be found in this book?

There will not be any universal recipes, buttons, knobs, strategies, and techniques for quickly controlling any bad behaviours, moods, thoughts, and language of an adolescent. As a collective, we are unsure whether such books exist, although some authors try to sell their ideas under such express titles. We perceive upbringing and education as a complex two-way process in which the constant participation and efforts of the participants are mandatory. The participants are individuals with complex spiritual, emotional, and intellectual baggage. Pushing buttons and knobs does not change anything unless you want to turn on a stove or a vacuum cleaner. It is all an awareness of the process and a desire for change that, after persistent two-way work and effort, can lead to spiritual transformations that will open our eyes to communicate as equals filled with mutual joy and inspiration.

Our experience

The book reflects our pedagogical experience with adolescents of different nationalities and the level of our spiritual development at present, which is the result of years of searching and personal transformation. It further reflects our observations as a parent of an adolescent and begins with our personal transformation and attitude. We hope that others will recognise themselves in this soulful conversation and that it will be a reason for reflection and a desire for personal transformations.

Upon reading the material in this book, it is an occasion to stop, think and change our attitude, if necessary, in order to learn how to build trusting relationships intelligently and happily with adolescents we may be caring for. It is a long process of mutual spiritual transformations, with the end result being the formation of harmonious and joyful relationships, of dignified, self-respecting new generations of human beings. It is worth the effort.

This book has been written with love, care and respect for children transitioning into adolescence and bearing the title of teenagers. As previously with our book, 'How To Raise A Hero', the material has been written in the language flowing from the heart.

TEENAGERS, WHO ARE THEY?

In a biological sense, children are all ages between birth and puberty, which is between 0 - 19 years. Typically, puberty is the time between the ages of 13 and 19 when children begin to change physically and mentally to prepare for independent life. However, this is all dependent upon the individual, as in some children these changes may begin as early as 10 years, and in some the upper limit is 20 years. According to some studies, there is a tendency to raise the upper limit more and more. Compared to other animal species and in view of their readiness for independent survival, one finds themselves in a rather disadvantageous position. It takes us an average of twenty years to learn how to function independently in society. We know that even after this age limit, for a number of social, cultural, and economic reasons, we continue to rely on our parents to survive. This is probably due to the advancement of various technologies and the improvement of living conditions within general human society, where many things are done for us, and we simply do not have to develop skills. However, we utilise our survival instincts, at least as far as finding food is concerned. In a way, this stunts our natural survival instincts.

The period of ages between 10/13-19/20 years is officially considered a transitional period. Some parents, caregivers and teachers may refer to this as the 'nightmare period', as children are extremely unpredictable in their behaviour and expression of emotions. During this period, they go through storms of hormonal changes that affect how they interact with the world around them. It is fair to say, however, that not all adolescents experience this period with difficulty, it is too specific and individual for everyone. In general, one can see that those children who are highly influenced and difficult to cope with, find it difficult to find ways to control their behaviour. This may reach extreme cases of the inability of adults to influence some children, but it is also possible to see children who are emotionally susceptible to influence, also experience the processes of change, somehow in a quieter and healthier way for them and those around them.

Adolescents can be a real challenge for adults who prefer not to remember that once upon a time, they were the same. However, through the voice of the adults, the strict society is already speaking, which is ready to condemn the teenagers according to the quick procedure, even quite often without any trial and sentence. Often adults are rude, too critical, too controlling, which is more often than not perceived by teenagers as invading their personal space and denying them the right to talk about themselves in the first person.

This transitional age is fascinating in that nature seems to have prepared a special program through whose labyrinths both adults and children pass. The transition period for the child is expected and laid down by nature. They find themselves in the vortex of many universal processes common to all living organisms on planet Earth. A teenager named 'X', for example, cannot oppose these general energy processes, because one may argue that their design is God's work, which resulted in them being a human. In addition, the evolution of cosmic intelligence, which decides for us. Therefore, instead of being angry with 'X' for not listening to us and spoiling the mood of reasonable adults, it is better to try to understand, remember and accept that our children go through mandatory development processes. This is because only then can they learn how to live independently and only then can they find their individuality, which we may not like, but it will be their individuality and we must accept it with respect and love.

Delicacy. Patience. Respect. Dialogue. This is what adults can offer teenagers.

This transitional period is as uncomfortable, strange, difficult, embarrassing, and unnerving as it can be a period of enormous creative charge, a desire for revolutionary changes, a search for one's own freedom and discovery of their purpose. Some adolescents may seek solace through altruism and humanity. This can be extremely exciting, inspiring, and progressive. As adults, we must support progress, even if we sometimes have to fight for it, and for our children, who can often be emotionally lost and misunderstood by adults and their peers. There are many and varied expectations, which may exert pressure, control, criticism, violence, and harassment towards them. Sometimes, they get more misunderstanding than unconditional love and acceptance, which acts as absent support for what they are going through.

Time. Attention. Interest. Unconditional acceptance. Listening to their point of view with the goal of understanding and helping them, not criticizing them, and distancing ourselves from each other.

This is a period when they discover not only the world, but also their place in it, and compare themselves with their peers. As their emotions are heightened, due to biological changes, they may become more sensitive and susceptible to criticism. Which at times, adults fail to understand why they have perceived the criticism so painfully. It is almost like a form of rejection for them, as they may fail to distinguish the difference between disliking their opinion and disliking them. It is almost as though things with teenagers are 'black and white', heated to drama, to maximalism and naive-romantic idealism. This is the charm of this period. If we understand what they are going through, we can skilfully guide them by the hand on their path as they see it.

Adolescents are aware that they do not have our experience, but they are ready to prove to themselves that they are not afraid to take risks, even if it turns out that they may fail. They are like birds that learn to fly against the wind to strengthen themselves. They do not have our fear that something might happen to them in this perilous flight, though we prefer to look upon them as little children, for we fear for them. The curiosity of discovery and the desire to find themselves as free and independent is embedded in them, this is what makes them take risks. The fear of adults comes from our instinct that connects us to them as parents, caregivers, and teachers, but it is also the result of our experience of what it is like to be a social failure, and not a single one. We have already been through this and know in advance what could happen and thus naturally want to protect them. On the contrary, this only deepens the gap between us and them. It is vital that their feelings and thoughts are heard and approved, and that approval comes from their parents, caregivers, and teachers.

Adolescents go through a hormonal storm almost every day for a period of several years. If it is normal for us, for example, to drink one cocktail a day, imagine how they have to involuntarily swallow ten or even twenty hormonal cocktails with various ingredients, some of which make them sleep, others make them irritable, and some tearful. Some cocktails have too much coffee, others are too sedative. They are not equipped to know how to deal with this chemical storm swirling inside them. Besides, they have to fight with the misunderstanding of the adults in their life, who are highly critical, inattentive, and constantly dissatisfied. This makes them aggressive and makes them withdraw and look for attention and love where they feel they will be understood and take their problems seriously and not as made up. This could be in the form of their friends, or it could be another adult who does not criticize them. Unfortunately, often due to their naivety and social inexperience, they can also run into people who will use and abuse their naivety.

Adolescents, even more than children, do not tolerate tyranny, control, criticism, and restriction of their freedom, including speech. They want support, understanding and sensitivity, and acceptance that everything that happens to them that concerns them is serious and should be heard and accepted with respect. In a friendly way, the energies of growth and development during this period must be managed delicately and carefully, so as not to repel them forever, but to support them in the direction of flight. This does not mean that they should do whatever they want, because upbringing and socialization are still related to the imposition and observance of norms and rules, i.e. restrictions. The way in which this is done is important, it must be in a dialogue and through reaching consensus, through methods of persuasion, not violence and punishment, on an equal basis, respecting the arguments of both sides. It should be fair to both sides and to give them freedom of choice, so that they do not become people who are tyrannical because that is what they see.

No, teenagers will not hear you the first time, not because they are rude, but because you are part of the outside world to them. They are absorbed in themselves and in the emotions, they are experiencing for the first time. This may be the excitement of the body, the interactions with their peers and the comparisons they make with them. Most emotions for them are confusing and they do not know how to control them. They think that everything that happens to them is for forever and therefore they rush to get into it, to experience it. They do not know that this is part of the development process, and nothing is forever, and emotions are our very fast guests - they come and go.

The changes in the body, the relationships with the opposite sex, the body upheavals caused by hormones and hormonal changes, the various moral dilemmas they face, is all part of a new world and a territory that consumes them with its intensity.

Therefore, their reactions are extreme and exaggerated, and as explored previously, they are sensitive and take everything personally, as an attack on their personality. Emotional balance is difficult to achieve and temporary. They pretend to be strong and flaunt a desire for independence, but they are actually very fragile and vulnerable inside. They are still just children, transitioning into a 'new normal'.

They discover the world and society for themselves in their own way and with their own rules. If as adults, you are not aligned with their version of the world during their transitional ages, then they may cut you out of it and you will lose your access to them. With teenagers, everything is dramatic and extreme, they vigorously resist anything that limits their freedom, criticises them or compares them to their peers. The very fact of comparison is humiliating for them because they are only outwardly self-confident, and inwardly vulnerable.

When the adult's desire to control and dominate the children is stronger than the adult's desire to know and like them, it is a signal that the adult has a problem within themselves. However, children do not come to their families as teenagers, they come there in most cases as babies. This means that the adults have already had 10-13 years to build respectful relationships. They do not begin their relationship with their children when they are 13 years old, but simply continue it, learning some specifics of growth.

THE CHANGES
IN THE BODY

Raising and educating an adolescent is no easy feat, because adults are faced with an entire new world that is both physically and mentally changing rapidly and constantly. A planet that does not understand what is happening and has no idea where gravity is pulling it and is therefore unable to control itself. It cannot control the changes that occur in its physical body, which are nevertheless visible and progressively more easily noticed. Often it is even more difficult to control all the emotional changes and waves in which it finds itself and most of the time it does not understand where they appear and why they influence it so strongly and where they lead it. The adolescents are in control of nothing because they are in a state of rapid self-discovery, which at times can be very confusing.

This is where the role of the adult comes into play, whether it be at home or at school, adults are the ones who have to explain to children the changes that may be happening to them. This period always seems to catch us off guard and we somehow spend more time resisting the idea that it has happened for our children, rather than accepting it, making sense of it, and changing our attitude and role henceforth in the lives of the children. This applies to all adults, inclusive of parents, caregivers, and teachers. They all feel some kind of idealised nostalgia for childhood, both their own and that of their children and students. This is also due to the fact that children, before entering the transition period, are more susceptible to control and manipulation. In that they more easily succumb to suggestions and more easily trust adults. In many cases, adults are those heroes that children want to emulate and are proud of, but also fear at times. This is still an age when you can both easily charm them and easily scare them. However, this does not last long, and then the adults seem to fall into an absurd state where they refuse to accept that their children continue to grow and develop in a way that is already beyond their control. This affects both the pride of adults and the hard-to-overcome illusion that they own the children, that the children belong to them in body and spirit, and that they must be at their disposal and under their command at all times. Overcontrol and obsession can easily turn into tyranny. It is strange that in this regard adults do not want to be honest with themselves, because if someone else behaves so despotically with them, then they will protest. Yet, we hypocritically refuse to recognise that children also have the right to protest.

The transitional age of children is a very fragile age that makes them vulnerable in many ways. Children have a great need for understanding, from an adult or a trusted person who, without constantly criticising them, is nearby to come to help if needed, but is also not intrusive. This is so that the child feels that he is trusted, and it can continue to take independent steps and discover its own directions. The only way for adults to deal with the challenges of this age is to know all about them and be prepared for them. Physical changes in adolescents occur due to changes in their hormone levels.

Changes in the body vary depending upon gender. For example, if the child is a girl, she may be extremely fearful, when first time has bleeding related to menstruation. Some children may think that they are dying as a result of the bleeding. However, with care, delicately and with concern, the adult should have a conversation in which to explain and assure that this is not the end of life, but the beginning of an exciting adventure in the world of adults. It is good that these conversations become a tradition, and it will be even more effective if, long before this age of the first physical mark, adults regularly hold educational conversations with the child about what lies ahead. In this regard, understanding is required, both from the family and from the school.

The most common physical changes are:

- Girls starting their menstrual cycle.

- Girls develop breasts, which can be uncomfortable at first.

- Girls are becoming more aware of their figure.

- Boys' voices grow deeper, and their faces grow hairy. This is the most noticeable change that happens to them during adolescence.

- Acne is a major problem for teenagers. Their entire face is covered with pimples and no amount of comforting and well-intentioned assurances that they are beautiful can make them accept their pimpled face with ease.

- Adolescents gain muscle mass. Sometimes this leads to excess body weight and may also result in increased body odour.

All these first physical changes in a few years will turn out to be extremely exciting for children, and here there is no middle ground. If the physical changes   are extremely pronounced, or if they are not very pronounced, may cause children to be ridiculed at school, as they move through the transition phases. This in turn can affect their self-esteem and can make children insecure, particularly if they are shy by nature, it can shut them off from others too. An adult must be constantly present in the life of children, to have access to their world, and to not let them isolate themselves.   It is crucial to talk to children and explain to them that everything that happens to them is normal, it will not last their whole life. Reassure them that everything is temporary, and everything will continue to change, but they should like themselves as they are now.

At this age, appearance and how they look, is very important to them. It can be the cause of dramas, or it can be the reason for easy wins amongst the rest of the group, if nature has gifted them with a pleasant appearance. They often have worries about their appearance, worrying that no one likes them, questioning whether they are too fat or too thin. This can then lead to the thought of exhausting diets, which in extremes can cause mental health problems. They spend too much time getting their hair done right, having the hairstyle that is popular at the moment in their group, choosing the right outfit and accessories. A derisive comment from others can embarrass and emotionally scar them.

For some children, how they look, their physical image, and how they are perceived by their classmates is crucial. For you it might just be a hair, and you may question what the big deal is. For them however, it is a source of self-confidence and individuality. Never underestimate their problems and the fact that something is a problem for them. If you laugh at them, they will refrain from sharing with you, and that can be fatal if they find themselves in a situation where they need your help.

This is a time of experiments with appearance, a time of diets, of searching for one's own image that needs approval. They need your approval, but also the approval of the group and class at school they are in or choose to belong to. Only, the approval of the adult is no longer enough, because the child opens up to the world as an individual person who takes his first timid steps towards independence.

Conversations about gender differences should accompany conversations about first sexual interests and how to accept body's sudden rush of affection as a sign that they are developing normally, and that nothing needs to be done in this direction. The child needs to hear these reassuring messages from the parents because the pressure from their classmates may be immense. Sometimes children force themselves to do things that they do not want to, that they fear and that they internally resist, just because they do not want others to think of them as 'socially inadequate'. For example, part of it is all about the interest in early sexuality today. Most kids are really convinced that they have to kiss someone of the opposite sex at all costs. This is what they suggest to each other, and it is a kind of sign of maturation for them. However, they also need to hear the opposite of this opinion - that nothing fatal will happen to you if you don't kiss someone of the opposite sex by the end of secondary school, and that it does not matter what other people think, what matters is how you feel about this. They do not have to give into peer pressure of their social group that they are in.

This is the exact time when the adult should do everything possible to become a friend to their child. In school, it is a bit more complicated, because of the professional distance that teachers have to keep. No, they are not the children's friends, they are their teachers. However, there are so many occasions that can be used by adults to explain to children, to talk to them, to share different points of view about what excites them and to illustrate to them the real-life examples. It is important that children have more information so that they are not left solely under the pressure of their classmates and friends.

Physical changes should be accepted calmly, new transformations should not be a reason for dramas, but should be adapted to them. A positive attitude towards our external image, as it is, is important for our self-esteem. At the same time, not our image through the eyes of our classmates, who can be mercilessly critical, no, our image through the eyes of nature, which always strives for perfection.

Encouraging children to exercise and eat healthy can be a way to boost their self-esteem because it is a way for them to prove to themselves that they have the will and discipline to take care of their bodies. A body is the home of our soul, emotions, and thoughts. No one else would take better care of our body than us. This is the key to good health and fitness, to proving to ourselves that we are in control of much of our lives. Children need to hear such thoughts and reasoning from adults so that they become a part of themselves.

Adolescents are often vulnerable, both emotionally and physically. Without proper nutrition and health care, they are prone to various diseases. They often have busy schedules, and between classes they do not have time to rest and eat properly, and therefore do not get enough nutrients. Fixating on how they look can lead teenagers, especially girls, towards eating disorders. They worry about their appearance and weight, and start following different types of diets and trends, which can often lead to mental health problems such as Anorexia or Bulimia. Stress at school is also one of the causes of loss of appetite or insomnia.

On the other hand, a lack of healthy diet

and physical activity often leads to obesity. This happens, for example, when the child eats high-calorie foods, fast food, and carbonated drinks. Obese children are also at much greater risk of lifelong health problems, such as diabetes, arthritis, cancer, and heart disease. They may also struggle with issues related to how their body looks or develop eating disorders as an unhealthy way to change their appearance. Parents are not always aware of these problems. Studies show that parents do not recognise when their children are overweight, for most parents it is important that they are fed. Without going to extremes, it is important for adults to monitor whether children eat healthily, because it is adults who create children's eating habits. Make sure your teen is getting the right amount of nutrients. Take care of a balanced diet for your child. Provide them with emotional and physical support. Realising that you are there for them unreservedly and unconditionally, without criticising them, but accepting them as they are. In doing so, this may help them to cope with various difficulties that they may be going through, whether it be at home or school.

NO ONE UNDERSTANDS ME

This is probably a common line utilised by many to describe themselves, and undoubtedly there may be some truth to this. This is because everyone has moments when they feel as if no one can understand exactly what is going on in their soul, thoughts, and emotions. At some point, everyone finds themselves in similar situations where they feel misunderstood. Sometimes that is true, but sometimes it is also a pose to show the world that our uniqueness deserves more understanding and sensitivity. It would not be an exaggeration if we say that this is the line under which the entire transitional period of children passes. Changes in hormonal levels cause not only physical, but also emotional changes in adolescents.

Teenagers are overly emotional, and this is also related to hormones. This confuses them. Literally anything can make them happy, sad, or angry and they can often be vulnerable and then cry. Quite often they do not know why their reaction is crying. Frequent mood swings are characteristic of both boys and girls. Physical changes prompt self-reflection in adolescents. Children who 'hit puberty' early may feel strange, confused, or different. In adolescence, children often become aware of their own inferiority or, conversely, superiority over others and can often be related to how their body looks. During adolescence, children often have thoughts about sex. They begin to feel the first different rushes of affection in their body. This can make them feel guilty.

This is a time of extreme emotional states that change quickly and at times, children are not able to make sense or control them quick enough. Their moods are susceptible to momentary experiences that are dramatized to the point of hysterics at times. They do not know how long they will continue to feel what they feel. They are also unable to recognise real from fake feelings and emotions. They do not know themselves. For them, everything that happens to them is experienced seriously and its importance is exaggerated, because this is also a way to declare for themselves as individuals with the right to feel what they feel. A feeling of inferiority and lack of confidence, shyness are common conditions, sometimes caused by their physical appearance or more precisely by the fear of whether the rest of the group will accept them. In addition, they may also question whether they will receive their approval or not. However, there are also adolescents with increased self-esteem and a sense of superiority over others. Often this is an occasion for some to bully others that are more timid and shy, thereby asserting their status as leaders in the group.

They often feel guilty for a number of reasons brought on by adults. Guilt and criticism are the two dishonest weapons in the hands of adults, with the help of which they sometimes drive teenagers to madness. There are countless demands and pressures on children in this period, expectations that they should react like adults and develop a sense of responsibility. The over-expectations of adults can cause them over-anxiety, whether they will meet these expectations, this related to the expectations of them for high academic results, subjecting them to constant stress and fear of failure. This causes them to accumulate anger within themselves, which sometimes erupts and sometimes accumulates in them, affecting their behaviour. This can transform into aggression and oppositional defiant behaviour. Some become apathetic and indifferent to everything around them that is negative towards them, criticises them and disapproves of them. This leads to passivity and isolation. Poor academic performance can also reduce adolescent motivation, as they develop an attitude that they are not good enough. This occurs when they are constantly criticised, they begin to internalise these feelings, believing that whatever they do is still not good enough. Praise them more often. Eating disorders are also associated with psychological problems related to low self-esteem and the desire to change one's appearance in any way. From here, the step to developing anorexia or bulimia is very small, and this can be life-threatening for a child.

They often feel lonely, misunderstood, and this in turn can lead to Depression. It is no secret that suicide among teenagers has the highest rate. Studies show that about 50% of mental disorders that affect adults begin around the age of 14. One-third of teenage deaths are due to suicide due to depression. Therefore, if your child is prone to frequent mood swings, if it suffers from insomnia or loss of appetite, you should seek the help from a specialist.

Changes in sleep patterns, eating habits, decreased interest in normal and healthy activities, lower grades in school, and preferred isolation are early signs of depression. The increased performance requirements, comparisons, and competition with friends, can also lead to unwanted stress. Being alert to these signs early on can help block and stop further damage, guiding them to healthy ways to deal with their worries.

Spending too much time on electronic devices can prevent young people from doing personal activities with their peers, such as sports, which can help protect against depression. They also experience new states such as 'fear of missing out', which further leads to feelings of loneliness and isolation. Depressive disorders are treatable, but it is important to seek professional help. If your teen seems withdrawn, has a change in sleep patterns or begins to perform poorly in school, then make an appointment with the doctor or contact a mental health professional. Do not delay getting help for your child if you notice these symptoms.

The most important thing adults can do for their children is to accept them as they are, especially when they are changing and are in transition. This period may be of different duration or intensity for everyone, but sooner or later it ends. Adults should be close to their children, show sensitivity, delicacy, and respect. It is extremely important not to underestimate what your child is feeling. Very often adults refuse to understand and accept that children have problems too. Small, invisible, insidious conditions that can be provoked by subjective, but also by objective reasons, from the outside world. Adults may expect their children to have problems of global proportions and only then recognise them as problems. Nevertheless, their refusal to believe, to take seriously the concerns of teenagers, is the first step in the child turning away from the adult and looking for another trusted person. This may be someone who will show sympathy and understanding, who will listen without being critical. Adolescence is a period of constant emotional ups and downs. You can help your child deal with emotional problems.

Therefore, it is crucial that adolescents feel validated in their feelings and thoughts because what they are going through is a real part of their lives. In fact, if their parents do not tell them, they themselves have no idea that their lives are going through a transition period at that time. This for them is their life as they feel and experience it. Anger, confusion, jealousy, inconsiderate attitude, dislike of their parents or elders, secretiveness, and high need for personal space, are but a few examples of emotions or feelings they experience. Challenging behaviours are the result of their inability to deal appropriately with the intensity of these emotions and exacerbate general problems.

Help your teen learn to take care of themselves, and that it is okay to feel what they feel. Encourage your child to play sports. Physical activity maintains the level of the 'hormone of happiness', known as Serotonin, in the body, which is responsible for positive feelings. Let them talk and express, whilst listening without judgement. Do not give them advice if they are not ready for it. Talk about how you may have felt at their age. This will help them to understand that it is completely normal to feel the way he does. Motivate your child to do what they like, as this will help them channel their emotions in a creative direction.

Although outbursts and mood swings are quite common in adolescents, it is not the only evidence of psychological problems in children of this age. Determining the symptoms of such problems can be difficult, sometimes requiring the help of a specialist. If you feel that it may be difficult in getting the teenager to open up about their feelings, then perhaps altering the environment may be an idea. A conversation could take place away from the home, at places such as a coffee shop, in the car or during a walk.

Listening to music becomes something of a religious practice for teenagers, which is because emotions are so important to them, and music perfectly expresses their moods, be it angry, sad, loving, lonely or rebellious.

CHANGES IN BEHAVIOURS OR HOW THE COCOON BECOMES A BUTTERFLY

Our specific actions shape what we call behaviour. Our behaviour is often subject to observation, criticism, and praise from other people. The rest of the people shape the society in which we move. It can be a large group, such as the society of a given country, but it can also be a mini society, such as a family, a school, or a class in school. In order for society to function and have order and discipline, it makes rules and prescriptions for how one should behave in order to be properly accepted, not rejected, or criticised. Compliance with rules is the form of control that society exerts on each individual in order to function in a civilized manner.

Adolescents with their specific actions often

challenge adults mainly because they often refuse to follow the rules of adults. Let us remember that this is the age that destroys in order to build. This happens purely symbolically, when the child is about to become an adult, a boring lawmaker like you, but for this to happen, they go through the phase of maturation. This correlates to that of a butterfly, meaning that just as a butterfly is not born a butterfly with the consciousness of its form of a butterfly, it passes through the symbolic death of the cocoon. In fact, we know from biology that the life cycle of a butterfly goes through four stages: egg, caterpillar, cocoon and then butterfly. Humans, as a complex energetic-biological being, also go through phases of development that are much more complex and complicated than the life of a butterfly. These include the reality of the physical body and matter, but also the tenderness and sweetness of emotions and feelings, the strength and endurance of the spirit, the immortality of the intelligent, wise soul, and the survival mechanisms that come from the blade of our intellect. It is so complex and builds on everything.

Let's face it, not all adults realise this, and we want children to be born with this knowledge. This is not fair, as they have no way of knowing if we do not teach them this, or if we do not explain it to them. As adults, we should demonstrate it through our own examples and behaviour, daily. If we do not do this, they will have no idea how exactly to meet our expectations of what kind of civilisation and society to build together.

Symbolically, teenagers are on a bridge under which there are countless dangers, one wrong step and they are in the abyss. In addition, on the bridge they meet characters of different nature, some are well-intentioned, and others are deliberately tempting and evil, whilst some are indifferent and confuse them with their apathy. All these characters want your teenager in their company. If you are not on this bridge, the child will choose the first character who lies beautifully and promises a lot. This may be a villain with a mask that your teenager will not be able to take off and expose, because of their vulnerability they do not yet have this social experience, and thus they do not have built-in survival mechanisms, however they are slowly learning them. If the adult is not on the bridge, the raging river below can flood everything and make the monsters below a reality. Then it will be too late to intervene, although it is never too late to show attention, presence, love, care, and respect. Be with the child on the way to this fabulous adventure.

During the transitional period, the child symbolically leaves to give way to a more conscious and mature understanding of its new role in life, to be ready to survive on its own. The transition period is full of challenges that children show through their behaviour. Unfortunately, adults are often quick to condemn behaviour in general rather than specific actions. But the specific actions are only the symptoms of the fact that something inside the child is not developing in the direction in which the adults want it to develop. It is like a disease of the body, in that first the symptoms come to the forefront, which is typically the pain we experience in different places on our body. Our instinct for self-preservation tells us that something is wrong, and we need to see a doctor. It is the same with adolescent behaviour. Behaviours are signals that tell us that we need to intervene with a conversation, an explanation. They tell us that we are most likely absent from the child's life, or at least not often present in it. We have already mentioned that this is a period when children need a trusted person who does not criticise and condemn them for everything, but one who takes them seriously and believes in their problems, however insignificant they may seem to us. They will withdraw from us if we laugh at them and if we measure the significance of their problems by the size of the planet. There are so many things that worry teenagers and that would show up as a symptom in the behaviour that prefers not to follow given rules, but with its defiant behaviour to attract the attention of adults.

It is no secret that for secondary school teachers, one of the most nightmarish parts of their job can be dealing with adolescent behaviour. Especially when they choose   to show rudeness, aggression, cruelty, forms of physical or emotional abuse, making up mocking names, ignoring, sarcasm, resisting, not accepting, defying, and sabotaging everything the teacher does. These are also signals, but not only that the child has bad behaviour and needs to be punished, but signals that indicate that a child's life is not happening in a direction that makes them calm, happy, and harmonious.

This is where we come to something we call the "holy triangle", which is formed by three sides: adolescents, parents and caregivers or teachers. The symptoms that the teacher notices at school and that may annoy them, because they break the rules, are symptoms of misunderstanding that the child probably carries from home, but they are also likely to be provoked by the school environment, by their relationships with their classmates.

We must be patient, compassionate, present, and caring, as we need to, as adults, make them feel appreciated and magnificent. Teenagers are accustomed to criticism and disapproval, that this is the first thing they subconsciously expect from adults. As adults, be different, be positive towards them, like them and tell them you like them. Paint them with positive words as you would like to see them. Gradually they will begin to meet your expectations.

Have faith in them. Just as nature has faith that the pupa will one day become a beautiful butterfly because that is its purpose, it is similar to this process, painful, full of obstacles, inconveniences, but the result is worth the patience.

At school, sometimes the emotions teenagers experience can be so strong, so much so that they do not know what to do with them. At times when they find it difficult to express, they may choose unhealthy methods to express, such as challenging a classmate to a fight. Sometimes to get rid of their anger, they try to self-harm or injure themselves. This can be very dangerous if not taken seriously. Self-injury may be in protest of something being said that they do not like, and because they do not know how to reciprocate, they try to self-harm to get attention. However, self-injury can be a form of self-punishment, resulting from guilt and can come in many forms of expression. Some forms include refusing to accept food, cutting themselves with a sharp object, pulling hair and other forms through which physical or emotional pain can be caused. It is not only pain that they cause to themselves, but it can also impact the adults in their world. Particularly because adults may worry about the well-being of the children that they are responsible for. In a school setting, challenging behaviour can be damaging and lead to a number of problems, both for the individual student and for their teachers and classmates.

Often, however, passivity, inertness, melancholy, and prolonged periods of daydream are a large part of their daily lives. Sometimes they can spend hours in contemplative daydreaming, which can often make school activities that require the exact opposite attitude, very difficult.

As a result of various extracurricular interests that are formed in the adolescent, this can also manifest in the types of clothes they may choose to wear. Different styles of clothing and hairstyles are often a way in which an adolescent may choose to express themselves, whether it is their general philosophy or opinionated position on certain matters. At times, such expressions of attitude may be deemed too challenging within a school environment, and thus can be perceived as a form of protest against the system and its rules.

Impulsive behaviour, often the result of a spur-of-the-moment, spontaneous decision, is characteristic of this age. Admittedly, adults may secretly admire the carefree, living in the moment attitude that adolescents have, as with time and age, every adult enters a routine which stands to kill the carefree nature. The desire for independence and freedom from the rules imposed on them by their parents and the school system, may encourage the adolescent to rebel or protest. Adolescents want to do what they want, as they believe their rationale is the correct way, without fear of confrontations or consequences.

The school environment is full of challenges arising from adolescent behaviour. If parents have at most a few teenagers at home, then at school there are several hundred and even several thousand teenagers gathered in one place. Just imagine for a moment the amount of boiling, conflicting emotions, passions, and desires which are raging at any given moment. An intense cocktail of emotions for sure. At times, adolescents can often be capricious and stubborn, unwilling to adapt their point of view to specific situations. When emotions are surging, with very little flexibility employed by adolescents, they may turn to negative methods in expressing how they feel. For instance, a fight may arise spontaneously, in the heat of the moment, which is eagerly enjoyed by others around. The peers of the adolescents in the fight, tend not to act as conciliators, but rather, as instigators who watch on with great enthusiasm and pleasure. They gloriously observe how the fighters exchange fists, and which manoeuvres they utilise on each other.

Commonly, when teenagers are fighting, their peers may join in on the action, resulting in a large group of teenagers brawling. When all is said and done, no-one seems to remember who started the fight and why they were fighting in the first instance. However, this is not important. The important thing is that they participated and gave each other primary emotions. In such mass brawls there is no winner, and very often it leads to a fatal outcome for some of the participants. Some teenagers feel that fighting is often a means of resolving insults, disagreements, and misunderstandings. Primary and fair - whoever wins is right. Adolescents truly believe that the right is on the side of the 'stronger' teenager, who often uses this right to bully others, which is unacceptable.

Disobedience at school can take many forms, for instance; ignoring the teacher's instruction, listening to music during class time, using the phone for socialising and playing games, being disruptive, daydreaming, looking in the mirror, walking around the classroom and refusing to sit down, regularly being late for class and displaying rudeness and verbal aggression. These can be sporadic or recurring and it tends to happen as a result of boredom in class and an unwillingness to complete the work set by the teacher. In essence, the adolescent misses out on their learning time. A change in attitude towards learning and a lack of ambition may be temporary things, but they may also be due to the influence of the company in which the child moves. This may be a choice of company for which academic success does not come first. This is when adults may need to intervene, because this can provoke the development of bad habits, which will then be challenging to change.

Unfortunately, parents often have no idea how their children are doing at school. When their child is in primary school, there is less of a concern, as it is very rare for their children to be involved in anything unpleasant. Even fights are very rare. On the contrary, in secondary school, as the elevation of hormones is in play, teenagers may behave varied in comparison to whether they are at school or at home. This may be a new side to the adolescents that the parents are not familiar with. There is also the concept that teenagers will often do things that their parents would condemn, all to fit into their social group and please their peers. An example of this may be engaging in collective emotional and mental abuse of someone, which may initially begin as a joke. They may make fun of their classmates if they feel it will gain the sympathy of the group leader, which they may deem as most important. Within toxic friendship groups, the adolescent may begin to change, and here another psychology framework comes into play; that primal and animalistic instinct, connected to our need for survival. Many parents would be shocked to know that their well-mannered and kind children can also commit such shameful acts. Children may often lie to avoid trouble.

So, parents, take an interest in your children's school life. Contact the school and ask how your child is settling into school life. It is important to be aware of their progress, so that as an adult, you can help if needed. Much of the disobedient behaviour is temporary and will subside. To correct an adolescent's behaviour, it is important to gain their trust, by talking and listening to them. Try to refrain from criticising them, as it may only make the situation worse. Remind them that they are loved and accepted, as often poor behaviour choices are as a result of feelings of neglect or isolation. Therefore, adolescents may be involved in activities, which are most unlike them to have any sort of feedback from their parents or caregiver, as many psychologists have pointed out. It is important to motivate them to always be themselves, and not conform to others. Remember that teenagers are largely dependent on their emotions and therefore they need your support. As they navigate through their feelings, help them. Communicate with them how you, as adults regulate your emotions, particularly when you are feeling sad, angry, or even jealous. Your confessions will help them deal with their own emotional problems. If you see that your child is in bad company, you need to intervene. Remember, however, that teenagers are sensitive and can take criticism harshly. You have to be more cunning and resourceful than them. An approach that includes shouting, aggression and insults cannot predispose them to a conversation. On the contrary, your aggression will cause their aggression in response. Remember that if an adolescent decides not to do something, then there is no power to make them do it. Therefore, approach them with kindness and care, as they will be more inclined to respond.

DIFFICULTIES IN SCHOOL

We have previously summarised some of the difficulties adolescents may face in a school setting but remember this is all very individual to them. There is a wide array of differing difficulties an adolescent may face. Metaphorically speaking, a school can be a place that resembles an orchestra, in that it is well conducted and plays a harmonious symphony, as there are structures and rules in place. However, it can also be a place where some musicians may struggle harmonising with themselves and with the other musicians in the orchestra. The school can be a joyful place of academic success, happiness, and positive friendships, but it can also be a place of academic difficulties and an inability to make friendly contact with others. The reason may be related to the adolescent themselves, but it may also be in the group that they are trying to filter into, which for one reason or another may find it difficult to accept certain people. This is especially true for newcomers who have to earn the respect of others.

With reference to group psychology within humans and collective behaviours, we do not differ greatly from behaviours exhibited in other primates, such as gorillas and chimpanzees in group settings. A classroom is characterised by a stable structure, in which adolescents with different characters, goals, behaviours and mentalities are gathered in one place. They spend a large majority of their day within this group structure. Their life happens in this group and their experiences depend upon the other members of the group, and these experiences are not always harmonious. Diplomacy does not always help to resolve conflicts and differences, and this is when teenagers take matters into their own hands and utilise physical aggression, which is not recommended. The reasons for conflict within any group may differ, it could boil down to envy, competition amongst peers, a desire to dominate or challenge the current identified 'leader' of the group, or disloyalty and betrayal to name a few.

The group usually has its own unspoken leader who sets the rules, but it is possible that the group also consists of several smaller groups that are related by interests and are relatively autonomous. It may be important to the adolescents to belong to one of these groups within the class and play into their search for self-identification. The more confident the teenagers appear, the more in demand they are and are able to manage to assert themselves and attract attention. All whilst the shier ones tend to gravitate around others and not intrude. The most popular in the group is not necessarily the smartest, or the one with the highest academic results, although this usually carries respect. Authority criteria is something that changes dependent upon what the group's common interests and goals are.

Friendship groups are something that teenagers zealously protect. In this respect, they are idealistic. Any attempt by parents to criticise their child's friends is perceived negatively and their sense of justice is highly developed. The adolescent may feel as though the adults in their world are criticising and disapproving of their choice. However, if parents or caregivers notice that a group of friends are having a negative influence on their child, they should intervene. They must do it delicately and respectfully, but with care and without prohibitions, because the child will do the exact opposite to prove to themself that they can make decisions on their own and can choose what they like, rather than what their parents like. There is the possibility that they may go against the grain. Therefore, it is wise to familiarise yourself with their friends, invite them over and get to know them. This will also help bring you closer to your child emotionally, as you are taking an interest in their world. Qualities in a group such as loyalty, faithfulness and care are exceptionally valued. However, actions such as betrayal, treason, gossip, spreading false things about others, false display of friendship, hypocrisy are not well perceived.

At first glance, it may seem that they are focused only on their experiences and that they are self-centred, but this is not very true. The friendships that emerge at school and that shape the groups in which adolescents move, are where they exercise all human qualities and relationships. It may seem to you that they are more interested in their friends than in you, and this is somewhat true. On the other hand, the children already know you and are familiar with you, so you, as the adults in their world, are also an important part of their lives. Additionally, it is also important for them to build something that will be independent of you and that will characterise and define them, something that they will owe only themselves. They are learning how to survive without you. This is also the meaning of growing up, as it is an opportunity to fly without being constantly assisted in this. Just like birds, older birds do not keep the wings of their young constantly.

Idealism, naivety, innocence, curiosity, breaking stereotypes, and taboos define a large part of the friendly relationships within the group. This is a huge constructive energy that can be used by adults for various larger social causes and projects. You will see that teenagers will be happy and proud to get involved if you can convince them and offer them a leadership role. They are not always inert and apathetic to everything around them. Much of this depends on the social environment in which they live and move, and on the values within the family as well.

Common problems related to the ability to learn effectively is poor concentration and the lack of ability of adolescents to focus on the lesson. Too often they are tired, apathetic, sad, experiencing love problems or bullying issues. Often, chatting in class with their peers seems more appealing and is more engaging and interesting than the lesson the teacher is trying to drag them into. Sometimes the lessons are not interestingly constructed, and this does not attract teenagers to follow the lesson with interest. It may also be because the tone, language and style of the lesson is perceived as highly academic and may be a barrier to the information reaching them. There may be a lack of desire on the part of the class as a whole to support the teacher, or the teacher themselves may feel no desire to make contact with the adolescent audience in the classroom. Therefore, this results in two parallel universes co-existing within the same classroom, at the same time. No one benefits from such teaching and learning. Exams often stress and worry some children so much that they may have panic attacks and become withdrawn and tearful.

However, the fact is that many teachers think that it is only their duty to teach the lesson, prepare a presentation and exercise materials, and the teenagers will automatically appreciate the work they have put in, respond, and participate enthusiastically. However, this is not always the case. Most of the time it is the teacher who has to make contact with the audience, and this can be done with an interestingly prepared lesson, with a good relationship established between the teacher and the class, with a genuine interest and concern on the teacher's part for the students and with an individual approach. Sometimes a conversation on a free topic may bring on an atmosphere and in whose conversation the students will be able to be present as individuals with their own opinion, rather than their social role as students. The individual approach includes getting to know each adolescent as a student, i.e. understanding their strengths and weaknesses that will help or hinder them in the learning process. It is also about getting to know each individual as a person. Without relationships based on good mutual professional knowledge, it is absolutely impossible to attract their attention, let alone maintain it.

For any relationship to flourish, it takes time. It is crucial to understand one's age and how they may respond to a particular stimulus, if we, as adults, wish to have a positive impact and effect on them. In order for them to learn something, enjoy their time at school and grow as individuals, we must take the time to understand them as adolescents. The teacher must make an effort to get to know them, and for them to accept them. This is because they are not just an actor in a play where the audience is passive and silent. The audience here is an active part, an unpredictable part and spontaneously destructive at times. This collective energy must be steered in the right direction and communicated intelligently and respectfully, or it will not accept you.

Kids today are different. They are not just more informed than previous generations, they actually know a lot before they even go to school. Which sometimes makes them wonder why their parents make them go to school at all. For many children, this is not their own desire, and their intentions to go to school are to avoid problems with their parents. This means that the school must become an interesting place that attracts them with more than what their phones and social networks can offer. Interest in their personalities and the desire from teachers to develop them can be a good basis for mutual understanding and spiritual development. Although, to channel the energy in this harmonious direction requires a lot of time and mutual efforts.

Adults also need to believe in teenagers, something that needs to be voiced. The lesson must necessarily start with motivational and emotional moments (phrase, joint song or sharing something). At the end, there should also be time for reflection, for them to share what excites them, a human conversation with them to realise the feeling they gained from the topic of the lesson, and how it shaped their understanding. All this forms the atmosphere of the lesson, without whose magical cover nothing positive and academic and inspiring can happen.

Many factors can stand in the way of academic success. It can be poor concentration and discipline, changing goals, competition, low success rate, lack of ambition, stress and tension, fear of failure, panic attacks, anxiety, and a whole host of other obstacles. In critical situations, when the demands and pressures on them are great, they may self-harm to draw attention to themselves or self-punish due to guilt. Their emotions are so strong that they do not know what to do with them.

At this age, there are high expectations for them academically, which puts them under enormous pressure at times. We may not feel that tests and exams exuberate immense pressure, however as adults, we have already passed this position and therefore it is an unfair way to think. When you are a teenager and have more questions than answers, things can seem pretty confusing. There are so many personal things that affect their self-esteem, and it makes them insecure. It is not uncommon at school to see a teenager crying because they may be afraid of the exams upcoming. The fear that comes along with upcoming exams, may be down to the expectations an adolescent may feel from their parents or caregiver. The fear that if they do not achieve the top marks, they will prove to be a disappointment for their parents or caregiver. It is the reaction of these adults, especially in cases where they have previously announced that they will not accept a lower score, that instil pressure into children. The child fears that they may withdraw their affection, that they may stop caring for them. No matter how much they strive for independence, teenagers realise deep down how profoundly they depend on their parents and do not want to be without their support. Parents should have realistic expectations and their ambitions should be healthy and aimed primarily at the good of their child. The exam grade is purely random. Your love should be unconditional, and your child should know that. Often exam situations make them experience panic attacks, and they feel as though they are suffocating and begin to internalise that they will fail anyway. Such children do not find much approval and faith in their abilities from their families. The family is the roots, and if they are stable, no wind can shake the child mentally. There are also cases when the child manages to cope on their own, but these are rather exceptions.

If adults are afraid to be honest with their children, let them at least be honest with themselves. Go back in time, see yourself as students, and admit to yourself how the pressure from your parents made you feel. Choose to be different parents. Love your children regardless of their grades and scores in school subjects. After all, each of our interests, hobbies and passions can develop to the level of a good professional career. It does not matter what their grades or scores were in specific subjects, as today we live in a time that offers more flexible and versatile opportunities for development. The worth of a human being is not measured by their results in subjects such as Physics or Mathematics. This is even absurd as a thought and assumption, and when this thought takes root in the heads of adults, such as parents, caregivers, or teachers, then they begin to set conditions for their love. Love with conditions is not love, but a mercantile account. Love must be pure and unconditional.

It is no coincidence that inertia, apathy, indifference, and anxiety are the main feelings with which adolescents associate their stay at school. It is up to adults to teach children how to enjoy school and be enthusiastic about everything related to school. After all, they spend a large part of their lives in school. It is imperative that adults must change their attitude to their work and to their life outside of work. Often, adults associate their work with tension, stress, fear of possible failures, and they subconsciously pass this picture on to their children. This is what teenagers know about work, they have a perception that it is a time of our lives that everyone rushes to then tries to escape and go somewhere else, where they could drink alcohol, relax, and not think at all.

Adults are the ones who should teach teenagers that our life is one whole, and it does not matter where we are at the moment, at work or on a vacation, it is still our life that we adore in all its forms. If children hear more often such a philosophy of life, they will also look at their time at school as a priceless time of their childhood and adolescence. It is a time that will never be repeated again, and therefore every second should be experienced with great joy and gratitude. Adults who hate the work week and wait until Friday night or Saturday night to go get drunk because they imagine that this is their real life, will unknowingly raise the same expectation for children they are caring for. Unfortunately, they will become the type of individuals who do not know how to achieve harmonious wholeness and how, in different places, to be themselves and enjoy their lives wherever they are.

A large part of the problems adolescents may face at school may be due to the fact that they have adults around them who do not understand their age. It may even be that they do not want to remember that age period and are too lazy and selfish to inform themselves. They are waiting for their Friday or Saturday night. Some parents or caregivers may manipulate children into diverting their attention elsewhere.

Completing homework, participating in extracurricular activities, preparing for tests and exams, experiencing personal dramas, self-doubt, exhaustion, self-punishment, are factors that may cause them to isolate themselves from the adults in their life. It is crucial to attempt to access their world to encourage them, help them, and come up with a plan together to overcome the difficult times they may be facing. Sports, music, and healthy eating are ways which may provide them with the strength, stamina, and vitality they so badly need to focus on their studies. If you notice that something is wrong with your teenager, then it is vital to consult a specialist. If you identify that they are overtired, distrustful, or unhappy, then once again consult a specialist. Joint walks in nature can fill you with optimism and help you outline your vision for the future together, may bring you closer to the teenager in your world and align your joint vision.

In group settings, there are times whereby adolescents are influenced by the aggression of others and may engage in collective bullying, as touched upon earlier. Often this happens because in the group the responsibility is collective and somehow their individual responsibility is blurred and absent. This makes collective bullying of someone more appealing, as horrible as that sounds. No one in particular is responsible. Everyone is somehow anonymous, and accountability becomes difficult to ascertain. Everyone is equally guilty and no one in particular is in the spotlight to be blamed. If the group chooses to ignore someone, it can be quite traumatic for the child who feels isolated and rejected. This is the first step towards collective bullying, which can be cruel and have great consequences for the child's psyche. The isolated child may perceive school as a dangerous place and thus may avoid attending.

In addition, harassment can be physical; for instance, when the victim is kicked, pushed or punched, allegedly as a joke, however, can escalate towards fatal consequences. Sometimes some bolder children, influenced by the social environment in which they live, carry their habits to school. They can carry sharp objects that serve both for self-defence and self-assertion. Troubled teenagers may also get involved in illegal activities and school for them is like an extension of their enthusiasm for the newfound activity. Adults should monitor and respond immediately. Therefore, children must have a trusting relationship with the adult so that they are not afraid to share, as this enables the adult to address any concerns present.

Sometimes teenagers may be afraid to share, because they see that teachers do not care about what is happening in the classroom or in front of them in the school yard. Often the control and mistrust on the part of adults is so strong that children prefer to deal with their problem alone, which can pit the individual against the group, and the consequences can be dramatic.

The school environment is not always calm and safe, although this is the first requirement and standard they must meet to be allowed to function. Although things may appear to be fine and calm on the surface, this does not mean that under the water things are not bubbling, raging, and sometimes erupting with terrible force.

Human interpersonal relationships are a complicated phenomenon. Science has long known the similarities in the behavioural patterns that fellow humans or other primates follow. These are patterns of behaviour, emotional expression, self-assertion in a group and the desire for dominance and leadership that are common to humans and other primates. We simply follow the impulses of our biological nature. In this sense, emotional bullying at school is like an extension of physical bullying, and it happens to be the leading one. Emotions for this age are a teenager's prominent mode of expression, which makes them quite vulnerable and sensitive to any kind of encroachment on their inner world. Their inner world is the territory they sacredly guard, but which is extremely fragile and vulnerable under the surface.

Emotional bullying has a wide range of manifestations, some of which are inclusive of laughing at someone, staring, and focusing on someone, following their every move, being deliberately rude, isolating and refusing to talk to someone, making up nicknames and funny names and highlighting situations where someone may have done something wrong, as an occasion to laugh at them.

New students are sometimes subjected to a full program of bullying, until they find their bearings and find a group with similar interests and behaviour patterns to which they can attach themselves to. One which can protect them from the bullies in other groups. School staff are required to monitor how newcomers are adjusting, and for any covert and hidden symptoms of bullying. In individual mentoring conversations with newcomers, they should be encouraged to share if something is bothering them.

Every teenager within a school setting will differ in some way or another. Whether it be with skin colour, another language, mental health problems, short or tall stature, good-naturedness and naivety and weight, all of which can be subjected to bullying. It is not known why overweight children are particularly bullied, but one may assume that it is because others see them as vulnerable and defenceless and unable to defend themselves. Overweight children really suffer because of the teasing of their classmates. Just as with other primates, the desire to prove oneself on the back of the weaker is natural and arises from the specificity of our biological nature. This is mostly an instinct for self-preservation and a defence mechanism, which unfortunately is sometimes used as a means of deliberate provocations. In this respect, humans can be just as aggressive and cruel as other primates, such as gorillas, chimpanzees amongst others. Battles for territory, control, and resources such as food, are fundamental to them. School life as a mini personification of human society offers a wealth of options where battles for control, territory, and resources are central to adolescents as well. Even more so in this age, when individualism and the desire to prove to others is heightened, it implies that your own ego and value are leading. Aggression and cruelty are both a defensive reaction and a means of self-affirmation. Some bullies may intentionally choose a 'weaker' victim and assert themselves, mocking them publicly at times. Behaviours such as this result in more sensitive children, who are insecure and afraid, especially the more shy ones who do not find the strength to share information and thus they close themselves off. Mostly, because they worry about the consequences of informing an adult about the bullying taking place.

The impulsive behaviour of adolescents can lead to serious consequences. According to statistics from the World Health Organization, 180 adolescents worldwide die each year from peer violence. The number of children who choose suicide over bullying are also not marginal figures.

Sometimes the tone of bullying is also set by the teachers, who should follow a professional tone in communication. Often, however, without realising and sometimes quite consciously, they define someone's abilities in front of the whole class. Teachers may be rude, exert bullying tendencies towards students that they do not like, making up names for some of their students.

For teenagers, such unprofessional behaviour on the part of a teacher acts as 'legal permission' to collectively open Pandora's box. Children should not be afraid to report such actions by teachers. Unfortunately, not only within primate groups, but in many countries around the world, beating children is still a common legal practice, executed by teachers and encouraged by parents. Violence begets abusers.

At school, adolescents need to feel protected and in a safe place. This is the first act of care for adults. For this purpose, prophylactic, preventive and educational conversations with children, whether collective or individual, should be held constantly. It should also be emphasised that we are building a civilised society, which is distinguished by following moral, ethical, and cultural codes. This is a concern for each of us. Creating a healthy, positive, and constructive atmosphere is the concern and policy of adults. Adolescents will follow them on the path to the light. This includes observing a code of conduct that is mandatory for everyone, both adults and children. It is necessary to teach children about how to cope with life, alongside school subjects, and also how to overcome their aggression, to deal with the anger that spontaneously overwhelms them like a hurricane and takes them down the wrong direction. It is mandatory to talk about the various manifestations of bullying and its consequences. Alternatively, constructive, positive, and optimistic relationships should be offered where everyone feels safe. Particularly where everyone is encouraged and inspired to develop their academic, as well as human, potential. Fear has no place in school. It should be a place of joy, laughter, and creative flights of imagination.

THE DANGEROUS TEMPTATIONS OF SOCIETY

This is a time of great experiments and discoveries. The time where you want what you do not have and what you do have feels boring and uninteresting. It is probably a typical human trait to always strive for what we do not have and expand. However, if adults have already learned how to control themselves when it comes to experimenting and embarking on unknown and unfamiliar adventures, it is important to recognise that teenagers are still learning, and for them it can be associated with dangers.

Teenagers are often not aware that they are in transition unless an adult tells them and explains, as they just follow their impulses, in every sense. The family and the territory of their house are already known to them, and for them it is time to explore what lies beyond the walls of the native home. It is nature that enhances their curiosity as explorers and discoverers of new spaces and impressions. Some of these new discoveries will be inspiring and push them to develop their creative and intellectual energy, which may lead towards good academic results, but also to the formation of creative products. It is known that many at this age begin to make their first attempts at writing, which may be expressed via poems and stories. Others embark on musical experiments, and this transpires from a hobby into a strong passion that helps them express their emotions to the fullest. Many become engrossed in painting, tourism, scientific research, which leads them to discover the fascination of philosophical debates and discussions of various eternal moral and intellectual topics. If the energy of their curiosity pushes them in that direction, then adults can be rest assured that they have done their part well.

However, the dark side of our nature also finds a way to express itself. The energy of the dark side of human activities can be quite obsessive and destructive. This is the direction of development that is full of temptations, traps and dangers that really affect both a teenager's physical and mental health. Yet again, here is the role of the adults, to prevent infatuation with a number of temptations, which at this age seem like an expression of breaking the framework. A protest against boring norms.

Adolescents are easily influenced by bad examples, because they find them interesting, as they differ from the daily routine. They give them extraordinary sensations, combined with the realisation that they are doing something considered forbidden and harmful, which can increase their adrenaline to the maximum. The search for strong sensations and experiences is all part of the initial impulse. Another reason behind influence is the company one keeps. These may be youngsters from the same school or new acquaintances outside the school. Some of the most dangerous hobbies at this age, which every parent worries about, are smoking, alcohol and drug use, participation in gangs or even carrying weapons such as knives. It may also include radicalisation, extremism and participation and belonging in youth subcultures that can even encourage suicide.

Often when influenced, teenagers may try cigarettes, alcohol, or drugs under peer pressure. A propensity for risky behaviour encourages many to try substances even before reaching adulthood. A sudden thrill or burst of adrenaline may result in an addiction or habit. For example, if a teenager has a parent who smokes or drinks alcohol, then they may view them as a role model to do the same. However, it is important to note that not all children follow in the footsteps of their parents or caregiver, whether positive or negative. Low self-esteem or the desire to look 'cool' may lead them to misuse substances. If alcohol or cigarettes are readily available, then easily influenced teenagers will be tempted to try them.

It is important to talk to children about the risks of underage drinking. Educate them about the dangers, including the fact that alcohol can have a serious impact on a teenager's developing brain. Also, do not be shy about expressing your disapproval of underage drinking, as this may make a big difference in whether your teenager decides to drink.

According to some studies, Marijuana use exceeds cigarette use amongst some adolescents. Among them, the opinion is even spreading that Marijuana is less harmful than in the past. This may be due to the fact that news is constantly informing us of the creation of new laws that legalise Marijuana use. They need to know that alcohol and drugs can seriously endanger both their lives, but also affect their mental development.

Medicines should also be added to the group of harmful and dangerous substances. This includes those that can be bought over the counter and also those prescribed by prescription. Particularly as teenagers may exchange these with one another. In addition, teenagers may be open with one another about particular substance misuse and their emotions. If adults do not inform them that this is dangerous practice, then they will likely be unaware of the dangers of trying medication belonging to their peers without medical advice. These risks should be discussed with them periodically, as well as the risks of drug overdose.

Parents or caregivers should be alert to notice any changes in their child's behaviour. Usually, if a teenager has started taking alcohol or drugs, then it will inevitably affect their daily routine, habits, and general behaviours, some of which includes their treatment of you. Loss of appetite, loss of sleep, unusual jerkiness, and sudden changes in mood, should encourage you to talk calmly and understand what is happening to the teenager. It is important to establish the type of friends they hang out with and whether the negative influence is not due to them. Very often, teenagers start drinking alcohol as a joke, so that others do not think they are 'socially awkward', which usually takes place at parties and youth gatherings of various types.

That is why it is so important to build a trusting relationship with your child so that they are not afraid to share with you, because they may not always be aware of the danger. Encourage them to be honest and share their thoughts with you. Talk to them about their problems and in case of emergency, one should seek medical attention. There is plenty of literature and video material on how to proceed in such cases, be informed and be nearby if they need your help.

This is the age when everything is still very fragile, their own self-esteem and self-confidence are very easily affected by what others think of them. During this age, authority figures change quickly, and temporary authority figures have great power over how adolescents perceive themselves. This positive or critical evaluation can be crucial. They may then become disillusioned with them and seek new idols. Disappointment can happen due to idealism and sensitivity, which makes them build up a 'perfect' image, which in reality cannot be covered. This is a sufficient and serious reason to break your relationship with someone.

New authorities can be inspiring and provoke them to become ambitious and constructive, but it can also be just the opposite, they can be destructive to their fragile confidence. The media and the image of role models, peer pressure, or more precisely what is fashionable in the group in which the adolescent moves, are deciding factors for the adolescent. The pressure from others, feeling pressured to do something against their will, to dress like the group for acceptance, can be extremely difficult and overwhelming at times. They are faced with the dilemma of being like the others in the group in order to fit in, or doing what they like at the risk of not being accepted by any group. This can in turn lead to their isolation. Loners who have the courage to go it alone are not always looked down upon. Often, such outsiders are bullied in order to prove to them that they are no different from others and there is no need to flaunt their different individuality. Bullying is also part of the pressure of the group to humiliate the individual and make them recognise and succumb to the 'power' of the group. Adults should be aware of who their child spends time with and the activities they are involved in. It is important to not treat it like a police interrogation, but as though you are having a conversation with your personal best friend. Be intelligently curious, be respectful. If the child does not want to share, then do not brutally force your way into getting an answer. You probably will not get any response, out of spite, particularly because the teenager may view your methods as disrespectful and rude. Rather, respect their free choice not to trust you and be around. If you have never had such trusting conversations previously, then the child may feel strange and awkward to share. Gaining someone's trust takes time and with small steps, beautiful, gentle, and delicate, but steady in the direction of your child's soul, you can try to gain their trust. If you want them to perceive you as a person and not as an institution, then share things from your life, share aspects of your day, and ask for advice on problematic situations. It is only a matter of time before that warmth makes your relationship blossom, and they will naturally share with you. The police interrogation only repels with its brutality because they are interested in facts, not one's soul or any trepidations, premonitions, fears, hopes or confused despairs.

Pressure from others in the group can lead to the initiation of various activities that otherwise, without pressure, the child would be afraid to undertake. There is something magical about the power of a group that stands behind you and supports you, one which encourages you, for better or for worse. It is precisely because of pressure from others that some teenagers begin to practice sex in order not to be left behind.

Another threat today, which compared to previous generations seems insurmountable, is the power with which the internet can bind the minds and consciousness of teenagers. Internet addiction is about to become an official mental disorder that affects both children and adults. Especially susceptible, are children and adolescents, who yet have not developed self-control mechanisms and do not know how to control the time they spend in various online activities. It can be different types of games or social media that they feel they must participate in to be part of the fashion of what is happening in their world. This can be aimless rummaging and searching for any type of information, abundant in pictures, sounds and sparse text. The indignation of some teenagers and the lack of interest in school lessons is completely understandable. Compared to this huge variety of pictures, sounds and colour that the world wide web offers, lessons are sometimes completely devoid of glamor and attractiveness. Lessons may appear as a mixture of being boring, edifying, with a monotonous voice of the teacher who delivers this information. It can make any teenager secretly spend more time on their phone instead of being bored in class. This is one of the reasons that teenagers attend school informed and expect something more from this place.

The online safety of children today should be a primary concern for adults. Adolescents often do not realise that with their photos that they upload on social networks, and with the personal information that they give, they may become targets of various unscrupulous individuals. Some who will try to abuse their naivety, gullibility, and inexperience. Often, complete strangers contact your child online and begin to purposefully recruit them for a cause or for personal purposes. They may present themselves as generous, understanding, or helpful, yet hold ulterior motives. Watch out for any signs of a change in your child's behaviour, particularly if they suddenly find themselves with various expensive items that they cannot afford. This should be a signal to you that new people have entered your teenager's life and you, as the adult, need to find out what they are in order to protect them.

It is true that with the advent of social networks, people have changed the way they communicate with each other. A large part of adults spends a significant part of their time in virtual space and they themselves consider this form of communication as an addiction. They realise that they have crossed the healthy limit of the ability to control themselves. Addiction to the internet, phones and computer games are also associated with some learning of new skills, however it is also a waste of time and a way to escape from reality. If many adults are affected so much and find it difficult to limit their access to the internet, then what is left for teenagers?

They can spend hours talking on the phone, chatting on social networks, or just playing games. Those of them who are overly addicted to the internet tend to have fewer friends and a less active social life. They spend their time in solitude in front of the monitor. Internet addiction also reduces the physical activity of adolescents. This forms an unhealthy and sedentary lifestyle. Internet addiction has a negative impact on academic performance because, in reality, when you play games for four to five hours a day, there is no time left for homework and studying. You feel exhausted from staring at the screen and from the pressure of following the movements of the game, resulting in no energy left to study. You supposedly did something, but in fact there is nothing.

Adults should offer adolescents with real alternatives to spending time together. This could be playing a computer game together, but with conditions. Rules must be negotiated that are fair to both parties but also offer a healthy variety. Nature walks or some kind of sports activity should be among the alternatives for spending time together.

Today, life is structured in such a way that it is not possible to prohibit access to the internet at all. Even to write and submit their homework, teenagers need the internet and a computer. If the adult tries to ban this completely, then they will be met with total resistance, because the ban itself is an unreasonable extreme measure in their eyes. The benefits and negatives of excessive computer screen time should be discussed and explained, especially when it is not related to doing specific work. How much time per day to spend playing games and participating in social networks should be negotiated, which should take place after work and chores. Work and play should have a balance. It should be monitored consistently for this. The adult should set an example of such a distribution of time. This can motivate the child to follow your example. The desire to achieve complete control, screaming, accusations, insults, and humiliations will not lead to anything positive, but will only make your child do things secretly. Try to persuade them so that they can come to their own conclusions about what is useful and what is not for them. They need to feel that they are making their own decisions about their lives, and not just obeying your commands. Thus, they will learn to be responsible for their lives and understand that every decision they make, leads to certain consequences that they must be ready to bear.

The group to which adolescents belong may consist of their classmates, but they may also make new friends outside of school. This is happening very quickly today through social media where they are looking for a way to pass their time and have fun. It may also be a way for them to escape from a reality that consists of perpetually disgruntled and grumbling adults, but it may also be a way for them to escape from the responsibilities that real life throws at them. Writing homework, preparing for tests and exams is something that stresses and worries them, while social media is entertainment and a beautiful, slow way to escape from all their responsibilities. They can stay there for hours. Bristling and curled up in a ball, staring at the flickering screen, from which some pictures or videos can be seen. They go with the current that carries them away from you. Much can be said about the benefit of standing in front of a screen in order to be part of social media i.e., to have a virtual life and friends. Even longer, one can argue about what skills are developed with countless computer games, through which they often practice activities prohibited in reality, such as killing, stealing, smashing, vandalism, and various other low-quality and anti-social activities. All of which are questionable moral messages. Often, they look for new friends because in real life no one around them understands them, or at least they feel that way. They may exaggerate their suffering and loneliness and the ecstasy of their joy. In general, everything is either up or down, but not for long, an average emotional state does not exist.

Online, they can also find different groups that are organised on the principle of interests, but also groups that are fans of a certain musical trend, football teams, or even an innocent patriotic organisation that is actually with a hidden nationalist ideology. It is also possible that they are an environmental group that aims to educate others, but also to carry out environmental actions, such as cleaning up nature. These currents and groups belong to the so-called youth subcultures.

Subcultures are a common part of every county and in every country, they follow specific cultural traditions. They arise as a reaction and rejection of the rules of society, but there are also rules in them, which, however, may be contrary to the social norms. In any case, they are an opportunity for young people to escape from reality, but also a way to acquire their own identity, different from that of others. Something that is cool, exciting, unique, original and that will fully express their great uniqueness. Such are the original intentions for participation in such groups. Curiosity, combined with hunger for something different and colourful, something not full of prohibitions, and something which will help build your image, movement, ideology or even philosophy. Rage with resentment towards social injustice, it is too romantic and an idealised feeling that no adolescent can arguably resist.

Through the group, they can learn to identify with ideas. This causes some teenagers to attach themselves to similar groups that represent different subcultures. They are characterised by their own style of dressing, make-up and hairstyles that are also often characteristic. They may have favourite colours, their own distinctive badges, and emblems, through which their diversity is recognised. Their behaviour is determined by the ideas that are held in the group. It can be exotic, alluring, but also dangerously aggressive. The style of clothes shocks adults precisely with the lack of style, and often teenagers look like beggars dressed in hanging rags. Yet this feeds into their charm and are not deemed boring like the clothes of adults. The make-up is profuse and creates a kind of mask behind which the true face is hidden and the new identity of an angry young individual rises to the surface. The accessories are carefully selected and are part of the group's uniform, may it be hats, glasses, chains, or scarves. Often such groups are peaceful, and their gatherings are almost a civilised event, so far as they can be defined as such, because the goal is exactly the opposite. The goal is to differ from the traditional status quo and to provoke. In other groups, however, alcohol and cigarettes are a common practice, which, combined with the aggressiveness that can provoke a large amount of alcohol, can lead to fights and other various manifestations of mutual harassment and humiliation. Sexual experimentation is a common occurrence in such group gatherings, and an unwanted and unexpected pregnancy can mess up their whole life because it will require maturity and responsible decisions ahead of what they may be ready for.

Each group has its own language of expression, often a jargon or vocabulary expressing the ideas of the current. Their language is expressive and naughty, unruly, its purpose is to provoke and to attract attention. Groups have their own places where they meet, these can be open places like a park for example, but they can also be hidden places that are not visible and inconspicuous, such as entrances, abandoned buildings, garages, or basements. All of which is not worth money that they do not really have. Today, it is often a virtual space where, hidden behind their anonymous avatar, they can have whatever identity they want.

For the most part, youth subcultures do not want to destroy society, i.e. social revolutions are not their goal, but their small personal revolutions, which may eventually lead to evolutionary changes. But in general, they are extremely sensitive to any social injustice and have a desire to change things. It is the energy of youth that drives them forward, despite their lack of experience and wisdom. This often leads them in the wrong direction, but their enthusiasm for change in general can be contagious.

A significant number of so-called 'difficult' children, or children from families where they lack love and understanding, often look for similar warmth in different groups externally. Often, they attach themselves to groups according to their social status, and this is also a way to adapt to something and to belong to some type of society. However, the criminal element, the fights, the drugs, the use of the new members by the older ones to perform various special services, can be long-term traumatic and give the feeling not of freedom from the adults, but of being trapped and harassed by one's peers.

Music is the connecting part of any band that has their favourite songs that express their emotions, whether they are tender, dreamy, angry, or sad. Music understands them better than adults and is like the therapy they need. They can travel together, go to the cinema, theatre, football matches or simply get together to listen to music.

The experience of the groups somehow complements the family experience, which is not sufficient, and gives adolescents a complete picture and preparation for the various manifestations of society. They are their way to search and find their identity. It is also about socialisation, and to learn to understand themselves better by belonging to a certain group, who act as a mediator between society and them. The positive effect periodically alternates with crisis situations and interpersonal dramas, caused by the still insufficient mental maturity and ability to understand others, and to communicate constructively. Not everything runs smoothly between the group members. They may fight, become disappointed with each other, and also with the group itself as a whole and no longer see the need to participate in it, somehow it is as if they grew out of this period. It is comforting if the other members of the group part calmly with the one leaving them. However, often they resent those who try to leave them, because it may mean that they have a choice, that they are not quite at an impasse. Separation can then be difficult and may involve violence.

Adults should be interested in the groups their children belong to, because this is a part of their external life which happens outside or in the virtual space where adults are not allowed. The right to privacy and secrets is sacred. Yes, they are still developing and do not realise the dangers that even participating in fan groups can lead to. Genuine interest on the part of adults and built trust will allow communication to happen at any time. It is difficult for some of the teenagers to leave such groups because they do not see for themselves their development outside the group, especially if they feel that no one in their family wants them and or understands them. Take an interest in their hobbies and interests. Nurture their interests with suggestions for joint visits to exhibitions, museums, the cinema, theatre, sports events, or music concerts.

Your child needs to know that they are your choice, that they will always have your love and approval. You effectively have their back and are part of a group that will never let them down, betray or leave them. This is the message every adult should send to their teenager.

Never embarrass them in front of their friends. Do not give away their secrets, do not hint at some compromising details in their lives. They will hardly forgive you if you embarrass them in front of others. It is as if their whole world and reputation they have so painstakingly built in front of others is collapsing. Communicating with the maximalism and idealism of this age requires delicacy, respect, and patience. Your love, concern, honesty, and loyalty will win their respect and desire for a joint dialogue.

THE FIRST THRILLS OF LOVE

Perhaps the greatest, purest, exciting and yet shortest love story in world literature is the one between 'Romeo and Juliet' from William Shakespeare's play of the same name. This is reflective of a typical adolescent infatuation. We, today, from the advantage point of knowledge that we have regarding human emotions and feelings in the twenty-first century, can debate about the depths of love Romeo and Juliet had. We may even refuse to admit that it is true love. But what is true love anyway? In any case, we must admit that there was a physical attraction, which by its force, confused children who were still inexperienced in this respect. By today's standards they are still children, although in the sixteenth century that was old enough for them to be married. The reasons for these early, almost childlike marriages arranged by parents are many, particularly the socio-cultural traditions of these societies. An additional reason may be the length of life, and another being the desire of parents from an early age to take care of the financial well-being and good life of their children by finding them suitable marriage-worthy partners.

At the beginning of the play, Juliet is thirteen, almost fourteen years old. Romeo was probably a bit older, although this is not mentioned. Their acquaintance lasts almost four days, during which they manage to fall in love, marry secretly, and with their inexperience contribute to a tragic development leading to the death of both. Everything in their story happens quickly, quick emotions, quick decisions, quick secret marriage, quick consummation of the marriage, quick death and all the result of some misunderstanding. If everything was not happening so fast inside themselves, they probably would have had time with a clear head to figure some things out, and both may have survived. However, in terms of literature, this love affair became memorable due to the tragic ending of their lives. Their youth and their inexperience are the cause of the tragic end. Romeo at first loves Rosaline and is unhappy because of her infidelities, but as soon as he sees Juliet, he falls in love with her and forgets about Rosaline.

The play is often described as a tale of horrors that parents of teenagers may possibly go through. In a few days, they experience intense things that others tend to take years to experience. They are too young, naïve, and eager to taste the forbidden fruit, driven by the lust of the flesh. They are maximalists, in that they love strongly and hate strongly, with no clear middle ground. Everything must be experienced immediately, as a hurricane of emotions and hormones rages inside them. They can neither understand them nor know how to control them.

One of the most embarrassing and uncomfortable topics of conversation between parents and adolescents during this period is certainly the topic of body excitement and the opposite sex. Many parents are often more embarrassed than their children and decide to avoid the issues related to the sense of sexuality and physical attraction that adolescents are beginning to experience. If adults do not talk to them about these topics and explain to them what bodily excitement effects mean, children will simply follow the urges and impulses of their bodies. They have no idea that there are still many more crushes and breakups, countless more kisses and hugs to come. It is important that they understand that they do not have to be practical when their body is signalling towards the opposite gender, particularly if they have a crush on someone. It does not have to be all consuming and based on physical relationships. Their physical excitements mean that they are developing properly, that they are responding adequately, and that nature is preparing them for their functions to be parents someday. At least that is what physical attraction tends to refer to in animals in the wild, for reproduction and the continuation of the species. Today, children have free access to all kinds of pictures and even videos that clearly show many things about sex education, and they are much more educated than previous generations, for whom this topic was taboo. However, they should know that rushing in this area of development can lead to unintended consequences of which the broken heart syndrome can be the most unpleasant part.

Adults must teach them what platonic love is and how to learn to transform the overwhelming sexual energy they sometimes experience into creative energy. Any relationship between a man and a woman based only on physical attraction is short-lived and limited. This is because such is the nature of the material and physical world, it is limited in its possibilities. Moreover, a relationship based on spiritual, intellectual, and emotional affection, respect and admiration has the power to last longer, as it can develop the lovers in their individual growth. This requires maturity and awareness of the nature of spiritual levels of development and adolescents do not yet have access to these levels. It is adults who are the ones that must prepare them for this.

Sexual energy also scares them because it is impermanent. Today they may like someone and are ready to fight a duel for them, but tomorrow their crush may be another person, and you are just as serious about your new feelings. They still may be unfamiliar with the fact that emotions and feelings are just our guests who come and go as they please and at times may make the teenager feel as though their crush is forever. Nothing is forever. They need to know that everything is changing, we ourselves are constantly changing and that the moment we tell someone the secret "I love you", it may not be true at all because it is born from the power of the moment. As their crush passes by, the feelings may go away. If adolescents are prepared for this side of nature, such as their feelings and emotions, then they will feel more stable and will not rush. This is influenced by their classmates, to experience at any cost the first kiss and the first sexual experience they may have. In many cases, children are confused, and even if conversations with parents are absent, they do not know how to behave and often give in to their momentary experiences and make physical contact. As discussed earlier, such impulsive actions may lead to unwanted consequences, such as teenage pregnancy, whereby they are not prepared to take on parenthood. They are often shy to initiate such conversations and prefer to get information from their more experienced classmates and from the internet. Unfortunately, often this information comes with unsolicited advice.

The best thing adults can do is take their children's problems, and their students' problems, seriously. This is because parents often do not know what is happening with their children at school, and they often have no idea that their children already have partners with whom they have some contact at school. Teachers often witness secret and not-so-secret stolen kisses and hugs that parents may have no idea about. Frequent contact with school is necessary for parents who want to get a complete picture of their children's lives.

As teenagers are experiencing fluctuating hormones and feelings of attractiveness towards others, they may idolise and have crushes on their teachers, particularly if they meet their standards and ideals. This can cause their admiration and affection. The teacher, who has authority, knowledge, and more experience, may take on the role of a 'protective hero' for some students, particularly if such roles are lacking within the home system. This is a delicate situation where the teacher's professionalism must come to the forefront, and they must do their best to keep their distance. Each school has its own rules and regulations on what to do in such cases, with one of the most important things being to respect them and not to abuse the naivety and inexperience of teenagers. Alongside it being illegal, it can also be an impetus for dramatic development. Therefore, it is important for parents to know their children well and to be aware of what is happening in their lives at all levels. In general, love experiences at this age tend to range between complete rapture or complete despair, there is no middle ground.

Everything can become even more complicated if the adolescent comes from a family that professes a religion that strictly forbids such early love contacts and does not encourage conversations around love. As a result, the adolescent, overcome by strong emotion, may go against family prohibitions, and follow the impulses of their heart, especially if their chosen partner responds to these feelings. The family in such cases often reacts authoritarian, which is not always the right direction. Yes, they can stop by force, threatening certain things, but that is not even half the problem. Adults are aware that these emotions will pass, such is our human nature, however they neglect to account for another factor. And this is how they have met the news of those first thrills. Was it with respect for the adolescent's personality, or with ridicule, neglect, drastic prohibitions, or even complete indifference? The adult's reaction is like an assessment of the child's personality. It shows how much you respect them as a person and how much you respect their right to feel the thrills of love, in the same way that you continue to experience them. Do you measure with double standards? We must be honest with ourselves; the physical nature of children is not their choice, but it is part of the cosmic design of higher powers, something that connects us to the rest of the Universe. As adults, it is our responsibility to prepare children for this part of their lives, so that they go through it joyfully and that their first love experience is not associated with nightmares and restrictions in the future. Love should be something that warms them and inspires them. Very often such the first love survives over time and can even transform into families.

However, if the parents tried everything they could do to separate the couple, then it is almost certain that they will not be a welcome part of that family's history. Often such parents can be driven by jealousy because they feel that their child is already separating from them and has their own life, about which they know almost nothing. That is why the role of adults is so delicate, in that they should prepare children for this beautiful period, to explain to them how to safely communicate sexually, if at all it comes to this part. At this age, they react quite impulsively, and if you are not around, they can embark on a number of sexual adventures without ever being ready for it. To also emphasise that the love part is only one side of our life, and in order to achieve completeness, they must still be ambitious and continue to work for their future, develop their talents in various directions and strive to achieve the best that they can academically.

Children deserve to have wise, well-intentioned, and fair adults around them, for whom their children come first and who will make every possible compromise, to maintain their relationship with them. Additionally, it is important to be a part of their lives, supporting them in a positive manner, and inspiring them in the directions that they take. It often happens that parents try their best to separate the couple, and sometimes they succeed, but they lose the love of their children. They are already afraid to trust them and do not believe that their parents really think about them, and for children, it seems that they only want to impose their opinion and decision. Allow children to not feel guilty for growing up and experiencing things that nature has built into them. Very often children feel guilty if parents do not approve of their choices and try to punish themselves. Our lives are meant to be celebrated, not to be deliberately inflicted with suffering and pain.

THE LANGUAGE OF ADOLESCENTS

What is the purpose of human language? First of all, for communication, as language connects us, and supports us to exchange thoughts, feelings, and ideas. Language can help people connect, but it can also divide people. Language can express our integrity, but also our dishonesty. It can convey what we think, but also what we want to hide. Through language we express our love, sadness, joy, anger, disappointment, pretence, distance, dominance, control, and submission to name a few. All social roles are also recognised through language.

Language is perhaps one of the first signs, along with physical changes, that we can recognise where the transition age has occurred. Adults often cannot believe how such a charming and obedient child, who until yesterday used only decent, delicate, polite, and appropriate words, enjoying universal approval from adults, now has an intolerance for these over-mannered words. The child may happily experiment with naughty words that make the hair of well-mannered adults stand on end. In fact, because adults react with shock, children may be more inclined to continue the practice of poor language.

By negation, you will realise that the time of rapid growth has come. "No", "I can't", "I don't want" are only a small part of the answers. They themselves do not know why they refuse to do something or cooperate with adults. This is what nature whispers to them and usually this is the first step towards independence and resistance. They are learning to say "no", loudly with confidence, as they feel this empowers them. If at this very moment, the adult wants to gain a "yes" response and starts insisting at all costs, it will likely result in a huge conflict, which the child will win. Instead, being aware of their age, take a pause and after a while, try again, but formulate your question differently, which cannot be answered with a "yes" and "no". The adult must be cunning, creative, and diplomatic. This is a great challenge for the mind of the ever rushing and tired adult. The child is in no hurry, believe me. So, this is your chance to develop intellectually to preserve your own self-respect as well, by not getting involved in useless conflicts. Adults should know these specifics.

The ability to say "no" is extremely important for our survival. It often takes courage to say "no" out loud, and children should learn this courage from a young age. Do we want them to become submissive and obedient people in the future who will easily give in to any more assertive and aggressive attempt to be manipulated and controlled? No, we want our children to grow up to be brave and proud people who have their own opinion and stand up for it. This should be practiced from a very young age. Our reply to their "no" should be - "I respect your decision; can we talk more and try to reach a compromise together?". No child will refuse this negotiation game because you are treating them with respect and like an adult. You are not ignoring them or yelling at them to get a "yes" result.

Breaking the language and not following the rules of grammar is the main thing that happens with the language of teenagers. All the stylistic layers of language that express disobedience and dissent and that lend a rebellious air are well accepted and used. These often formulate in the slang words that each group perceives as their own code and uses as a way to break the rules and norms to be different. Here the sign of division may be along social lines. Each language has its own youth slang, which is a combination of foreign language words and words of low stylistic colour. These may often be combined with obscenities. Censoring one's own language is what teenagers refuse to do, and they can use language as a secret code, as an attempt to provoke adults, because they can very well predict the indignant reaction of adults to obscenities. Using profanity gives teenagers a sense of freedom, defiance, rebellious excitement, and validation as something different from the adult world.

Failure to follow grammatical rules may also shock adults. The way teenagers write is greatly influenced by the breaking of language rules, characteristic of social networks and text messages on phones. Instead of whole words, a combination of numbers, signs, letters and emojis are used. Abbreviations that are obtained from the combination of the first letters of the words are also very popular, for each language these are different abbreviations. However, this does not mean that it is the teenagers who destroy the language. No, they just adapt it to fit their changing personality and the search for their new identity. Language is in a constant process of change, and we all participate in this, not just teenagers. Such is the nature of natural language; today's language mistakes are tomorrow's new language rules. Today's teenagers are definitely more dynamic than the generations of decades ago. This dynamic is also due to rapidly changing technologies and the opportunities they offer. Their parents or grandparents still remember the correspondence based on paper letters, in which they exchanged information long, beautifully, and politely. Today's youth communicate dynamically and briefly.

If we have to summarise, adolescents use language for self-affirmation, to exchange coded secret words, to increase distance with adults, and to protest. A common feature of their language is negation and negative constructions. Lies and silence are skilfully used to get out of dangerous situations for them when they are afraid of something. Using profanity can be quite an exciting exercise precisely because it is forbidden and indecent. Meaningful screaming silence is a strong form of protest, distancing, and dissent. In general, they are not inclined to participate in long dialogues, as they are perceived as something that takes them away from their precious moments of contemplation and a state of quiet dreamy understanding of the world.

We cite an example of a typical attempt by an adult to encourage their teenage child to pay them some attention. For this dialogue below, it is a mother who is trying to speak with her daughter, aged between 13-14 years old:

Mum: "Oh, but you smiled at me! You are such a ray of sunshine!".

Daughter: "Don't exaggerate though".

Mother: "Hurry up, as we are running late. You have been doing your hair for ten minutes".

Daughter: "But why do you have to make everything negative?".

Mum: "Let's go for a walk".

Daughter: "No!".

Mum: "We will only go to the end of the street and back".

Daughter: "There are clouds, it may rain".

Mum: "Ok, then we will walk for only half an hour, we will stay close by".

Daughter: "Well, if it's going to be nearby, then what is the point of going out? I'm fine like this".

Mum: "Don't you think it is a bit messy in your room?".

Daughter: "It is fine".

Mum: "I'll help you sort it out. Do you want to?".

Daughter: "No! Everything is perfect and, in its places,".

Mum: "We will cook something together on Sunday. You wanted to learn to cook, didn't you?".

Daughter: "If I'm just going to cut the vegetables again, I don't want to".

Mum: "Do you want to mix the ingredients this time and I will cut the vegetables?".

Daughter: "No!".

Mum: "Do you at least want to stir the dish?".

Daughter: "I'm fine like this".

Mum: "We can make some cake together".

Daughter: "Wow, is this my mother who is offering me sugar?!".

Mum: "What did you do at school today?".

Daughter: "Nothing!".

Mum: "All day at school and you did nothing, huh?".

Daughter: "Nothing!".

Mum: "Which girls are your friends at school?".

Daughter: "You do not know them".

Mum: "Well, tell me about them so I can get to know them".

Daughter: "And what is that to you?".

Mum: "Well, I want to know things about you".

Daughter: "Well, they are girls. Is that not enough?".

Mum: "What are their names? Where are they from?".

Daughter: "Are you even that interested?".

Mum: "Yes, I am interested. Do they study well?".

Daughter: "How would I know?!".

Mum: "What do you talk about?".

Daughter: "Nothing, we just have lunch together, eat and be silent".

Mum: "And you are friends".

Daughter: "They are in my friend group".

Mum: "Aha...".

Daughter: "Mum, mum, a boy in my friend group is having a party for his birthday and I am invited. I am so excited! What will I wear?! I can go, right?! Oh, I am so excited! Finally, something interesting happened in my life!".

Mum: "But I thought there were only girls in your friend group?! Where did this boy come from?!".

Daughter: "Oh, but he is from primary school, and he is like a friend to us".

Mum: "Sure. Well, I do not know if you can go, it

will be late. Who will drive you? I don't know, I don't know. Let me think about it and I will tell you tomorrow, there is still another week, right? Big deal, if you don't go, there will be other occasions".

Daughter: "I think I have the most boring life. Why are you so unfair and strict?!".

Mum: "Oh, how nice it is to stay in silence together. See what interesting things we found happened to you today".

Daughter: "You always exaggerate. Why are you doing this?!".

Mum: "Give me a kiss".

Daughter: "No!".

Lying is a phenomenon that can give rise to many problematic situations. Why do children and adolescents lie? Why do adults lie? Adults may lie for various reasons, whether it is to avoid conflict, to hide something, to distance themselves, due to a fear of punishment or maybe for a bunch of other reasons. For more or less the same reasons, teenagers also resort to lying. If we emphasise the harm of lying at this age, it is not to promise that when they grow up, children will stop lying. No, as adults know, we lie too. In doing so, we consciously choose to hide something, distort it, or invent a new reality. However, adults are considered more mature individuals who are aware of the moral and legal consequences that lying can have. Adolescents are not yet fully mature and responsible, as they do not know what consequences lying can sometimes have for them. This is precisely why we must be vigilant to teach them that every action has a counteraction, that every action has consequences.

Lies and silence are sometimes the only means left to adolescents. Their power is like a double-edged sword that can help save you but can also push you in a dangerous direction. Therefore, adults must learn to listen, not only to what adolescents say, but also to what they do not say, what they keep silent about, and what silence means. Prolonged silence and deliberate deception may be a sign that your child is in a potentially dangerous situation, both physically and mentally.

Adolescents resort to lying when they are afraid of punishment, when they want to keep their own and other people's secrets, when they want to keep their right to independence, as a way of self-affirmation. They also lie when they are afraid of failure, and as a result, grown children will reluctantly open up to talk about their first love thrills. The intimate sphere for them is an inviolable territory where many things are secret. Especially if the parents do not approve of their love choices and try to separate them, this is the surest way for this romantic story to turn into a secret heart story. It is then, when the access of adults in this sphere of children's lives will be forbidden and unknown. So instead of forbidding, try to create a relationship in which they feel that they are not afraid to share things with you, but on the contrary, that you will understand and support them. It then becomes a relationship in which you not only talk, but also listen, and becomes a relationship where children are not afraid to share, because if they are afraid of your reaction, they will lie.

At the end of the day, it is about your child, not the love choice that has yet to be changed many times over. There will be many objects of love interests, but you, who have more life experience, know this, and teenagers do not. Therefore, by creating barriers towards communication, you may encourage the child to behave in an extreme way, where they will do what they want, and you may lose your friendship with them as a result. This is because from their perspective and position, your disapproval means that you do not like their choice, and children struggle with handling rejection. Show the child that you are always on their side, whatever their choice is, whether it is right or wrong. In that case, you will have a relationship built on trust, not forced lying. It is all in the hands of adults.

Out of fear, teenagers may resort to lying when someone is bullying them at school. Instead of telling everything to their parents or teachers, they may withdraw into themselves and suffer quietly and silently, often denying the obvious. Even though it is obvious that something is wrong with them. This happens when children believe that if they disclose any bullying, then the bully will continue to bully them even more and get 'revenge'. It is crucial to reassure them that it is in fact the opposite and that they do not need to be afraid but should be honest and open about what they are going through and how others are treating them. Sometimes the emotions they experience are so strong that they choose to self-harm, but not admit the truth. When self-injuring, they often do not know when to stop and it can be fatal for them.

Therefore, the lie should be approached delicately, but also in a detective style, you should try to understand why the choice is the lie and not the truth. There is always a reason behind this choice, and you need to understand it. However, not in the harsh and authoritarian way with shouting and prohibitions, which will only push the child away from you, increase the distance and increase the lies you hear, which the child will already produce out of a sense of self-preservation. This may be an attempt for them to guard themselves from you and your anger. The approach must come from the heart and the leading feelings you feel must be love and care. Only the systematic display of love and care will open your child's heart to you.

Lies, fabrications, fantasies, pretences are all tools that adolescents often use to create a false image in front of their classmates and strangers, whom they want to please. Behind this there is also a manifestation of a certain creativity, to which they resort, when, for example, they are for some reason ashamed of their parents, their profession, of where they live, and fictions are then part of their desire to distance themselves from this environment. This shows there is still immaturity and a lack of built stable internal self-esteem and confidence in themselves and in their own strengths and capabilities, as something different from those of their parents. This realisation comes with growing up and maturing.

Sometimes these fabrications are not entirely harmless, and they are aimed at certain people with the intention of harming them. Often at this age, they experiment with the reactions of their classmates by spreading lies about them, causing the target of those lies to suffer. If you notice such a systematic use of lies and fabrications in your child, it is probably not a bad idea to seek help from a psychologist who, with the authority of a professional, may be able to explain and help the teenager understand how dangerous crossing the border between truth and lies can be.

Exaggeration is also a characteristic phenomenon that adolescents use quite consciously to achieve dramatic effect. They can exaggerate when describing an event or how they feel, and can completely exaggerate banal everyday facts, and the assessment they give of them can be misleading. They resort to exaggeration to get themselves out of a situation, to get the attention of someone they like, to be the centre of attention for a little while, whether it be to fit certain group standards, to get what they want, or to have fun. They may be perceived as 'cool' or the 'class clowns' in doing so, whose company everyone seeks in adolescence. There is a fine line between exaggeration and lying, and teenagers should be aware that they should not cross it. The same applies to your children's work area, their school. Those working in the field of education are professionals who are trained in how to respond to cases where a teenager uses language inappropriately. In such situations, each place has its own rules which enables clarity on a situation. Cases where the adolescent lies or manipulates others are also dealt with appropriately, following the rules and procedures in such situations. For some teenagers, this can be a terrible period of their life, which they will later remember with a sad feeling. For others, this period can happen in a completely different way, it can be full of successes and academic ambitions.

This is an age when you need to be careful and delicate, but not completely forgiving all of the time. It is important to be strict in certain situations. In school, the teacher is not their friend, but someone who must maintain a certain professional distance, although they are obliged to create a friendly and professional atmosphere. Teachers are to be interested in human terms, by understanding the students and ensuring that if they need the support, this is readily available for them. This is a very fine line that should not be crossed, because otherwise the power of the pedagogical impact will be weakened. The collective energy must be constantly directed in the direction of creating and exercising a positive, warm, productive, beautiful, smart, stimulating, creative and professional atmosphere.

In general, age is full of creative energy, which cosmic energy itself and all nature around us scatters in full force on children. Language as a way of expressing ourselves, is also a tool on how to hide, but also how to stand out, and to fit into a group. It is also how to avoid rules and regulations, how to show our individuality, who we really are and how we differ from others. It is also a model on how to be like others and use the formal styles of language to achieve academic results. These dilemmas are not easy dilemmas, they sometimes lead to a painful split that needs time to think through, understand and accept. It is also an opportunity for teenagers to learn about the different social roles we all have and when and what their appropriate use is. Maturity also comes with the realisation that we are one in all our different and seemingly contradictory manifestations. All our activities, such as our language, love, academics, friendship, creativity and even family, are all different layers of us. Realising this simple fact means having maturity and accepting ourselves in all the complexity and wholeness of what it is to be human.

The fragmentation of our personality, our perception that 'I only live when I am having fun but not when I study and work', or 'I use slang and colloquial terms, because I do not need to use standardised and approved language to succeed socially'. All this fragmentation leads only to suffering, rejection of parts of ourselves, pain and a lack of sense of wholeness for ourselves. We are everything put together. Growing up is a time when children should be introduced to this healthy philosophy of wholeness with ourselves, and also with the entire intelligent cosmos and nature surrounding us.

THE DIFFERENT CLASSROOM

The classroom can be full of additional challenges that, added to age challenges, can complicate the learning process. For some adolescents, the typical problems of age are combined with individual health problems or mental characteristics of their development, which they may be born with. As a result, they may need to make extra efforts to meet the standard expectations of academic success. Standard expectations for academic success are constructed for children who do not have medical conditions, that would make it difficult to achieve these successes. However, for children with Autism, Dyslexia, various physical disabilities, or even for bilingual children, the standard classroom and standard expectations for academic success can prove overwhelming. The difficulties are both personal, resulting from the personal diagnosis, adding to them age-related difficulties such as a poor ability to concentrate attention and to remember.

Depending on how serious their personal illness is, such children may be referred to specialised schools where specialists will help them adapt and succeed in the academic process. It is a long process that usually involves a team of senior professionals who strive to find the best solutions for everyone's education. Mainstream schools also have professionals who make sure that children with special needs adapt and succeed academically. Subject teachers are also trained to provide additional assistance and to change their teaching methods to be as useful as possible for children to learn the material in their subject. The important thing is that these children and their abilities in the individual subjects are considered individually and in view of their abilities, and not in view of the diagnosis they have.

Experience shows that among them there are both children with excellent academic abilities and children for whom school and academic success are not the most important thing. This is also the case with children who do not have special needs. Our experience also shows us that the teacher must master a variety of methods, but it is also psychologically important that these children do not feel isolated from others. In the classroom, they should feel like everyone else, as the teachers should always try to identify each child's skills. This will help the children to blend in with the others. Constantly emphasising that they are 'different', can have a negative psychological effect on them.

In general, they need more time to understand the learning material and more time to answer questions related to it. On the part of the teacher, more patience, delicacy, understanding, support, and ingenuity are needed.

Due to the nature of the book, we cannot dwell here in detail on the specifics of all the diagnoses that classify children as 'different' or 'children with special needs'. However, we will look at the specifics of the two most common categories most often encountered in the classroom, which are Autism and Dyslexia. It is important to also understand what additional emotional, and mental challenges and barriers they present for some adolescents. We will also pay attention to bilingual children, who may not necessarily have learning difficulties, but may still struggle within the classroom all the same. The very specificity of bilingualism is a challenge in itself in a classroom where everything boils and boils differently, but where most children speak the local language, which for bilingual children turns out to be a second language. For bilingual children, the language in the classroom is often not their mother tongue. The teacher must be a true professional virtuoso to deal with all this different energy, to be able to channel it in a different way, but in the end to be able to achieve academic results together with the children. Regardless of their diversity.

Parents, who often have difficulties with 1 or 2 children in adolescence, often cannot even imagine how difficult and sometimes impossible it is to be a teacher in such a classroom. Unfortunately, the work of a teacher is often underestimated, and it is sometimes equal to a feat.

We will mention only some of the most general and typical signs in the behaviour of children with autism, and with a view of how they may fit in the classroom together with others. Working with children who have autism is a challenge that enriches you as a professional because it requires you to expand your horizon of understanding, particularly about the diversity of human nature. Not all children diagnosed with autism are characterised by the same degree of expression of the signs, which is why it is important to speak about the autism spectrum. The 'Autism Spectrum Disorder', (ASD), covers cases with milder features as well as more serious disorders in the development of the brain. Autism is mainly expressed in a reduced capacity for social interactions and communication, which results from the inability to select adequate emotional responses to stimuli from the outside. The causes of autism are not fully understood.

One symptom is not enough to define autism, rather a characteristic triad is needed. This may be due to lack of social interactions; impaired mutual communication; limited interests and a repetitive repertoire of behaviours. Autism is a condition characterised by a predominance of a closed inner life, active withdrawal from the outside world and poor expression of emotions. A person with autism is not capable of full social communication and often cannot, like most people, intuitively feel the state of another person.

Children who have autism tend to do better in subjects that require accuracy, objectivity, following a clear structure and method. Mathematics is preferred by most autistic children, even if they do not show special abilities in this subject, as they are following certain rules. This reassures them because it requires objective logic and repetitive movements and intellectual actions. Everything about recognising emotions in others and responding to emotional stimuli can be confusing and stressful. Left to themselves to make a subjective assessment of a situation, autistic children feel helpless and unable to assess how adequate their choices are. In this sense, subjects such as literature, psychology, languages, and some others can be a real insurmountable obstacle for them. On the contrary, imagination, visualisation, metaphors and symbols, abstractness, and subjectivity, because of their dual nature, make it difficult for autistic children to know what is right and what is wrong.

Making and maintaining friendships is difficult, precisely because the subjective feeling of the other through emotions is an obstacle for autistic children. Eye contact is something some of them prefer to avoid. All this can lead to isolation from the world of others and to building your own inner world, which others hardly understand and to which they do not have access. They are sensitive to the evaluation of the outside world because it is often critical of them, and this leads to auto-aggression and a desire to self-punish.

They like routine activities that make their day predictable and understandable, even though for others this is a sign of monotony. Change brings an unknown that feels scary to them. Their interests and hobbies are limited and often require cyclical, repetitive actions. If they have to work in a team, they continue to behave as if they are alone and avoid communication with others.

Some studies show that auto-aggression is characteristic of autistic children who, in a state of intense rage, make attempts to self-harm because they do not know how else to resolve a situation in which they feel helpless.

Difficulties in learning material are also associated with a deficit of attention, which makes it difficult to concentrate on one thing, and to retain attention for a longer period of time. In some, hyperactivity is also noticed, usually as a reaction to tasks set by adults, and often shows an inability to cope. It may also indicate confusion of the order that the child has chosen.

In general, autism is the result of multiple developmental factors that affect the functional systems of the brain and its development. Some researchers see in autism a tendency towards over-systematisation, in which a person seeks to create their own rules for dealing with situations. The ability to empathise, where one must show emotions of sympathy and understanding towards other people, is not observed.

The behaviour of autistic children is characterised by limited social interactions due to communication difficulties and limited repetitive behaviour. Most children with autism lack social support, stable relationships with others, career prospects and a sense of self-determination. Friendships at school can be a real test. The lack of empathy for others can turn out to be more of a myth than a reality if it is developed, educated, guided, and delicately explained the need for it and the technology of its use. All of this can be extremely stressful and worrisome for them, because they take most things literally.

Autistic children may have difficulty reading non-verbal cues, such as body language or tone of voice, to guess how someone else is feeling. For example, they may not be able to tell when someone is teasing them or using sarcasm. In response, their faces remain expressionless and show no reciprocating emotion.

Older children with autism who realise that they are different from other people are also often aware of how others see them, and this can lead to a reluctance to gather with many people in one place. It may also impact their mental health and lead to problems such as Depression. They may also feel like outsiders. At school, other children may bully them because of their differences, making them very vulnerable. It may be difficult for them to understand what is happening around them. This can lead to a build-up of feelings of frustration that children cannot control at the moment.

In addition to children with autism, there may also be children with dyslexia in the classroom. Historically, in most European countries, the concept of "dyslexia" includes all problems related to written speech. More specifically problems with mastering the skill of reading and writing, literacy problems, problems mastering arithmetic, problems related to impaired motor skills and coordination and even attention problems. There is another type of dyslexia, which is referred to as letter dyslexia (lat. dyslexia litteris). It manifests itself during input in the form of a violation of the sequence of adjacent letters. It is impossible to trace the manifestation systematically and it appears only in words consisting of more than four letters.

In dyslexia, intelligence is preserved, but generally its symptoms are as follows; poor reading skills, error reading, guessing reading, misunderstanding of read information, difficulties in retelling the text just read, difficulty writing words, difficulties copying text, pronounced problems with handwriting, inability to complete the task on time, increased sensitivity of the nervous system, excessive emotionality, irritability, impulsiveness, emotional instability, impaired coordination of movements, clumsiness, violation of body posture, difficulties in determining the right and left sides, disorders of interhemispheric interaction, increased aesthetic taste, and a pronounced sense of justice.

Dyslexia is a learning difficulty that primarily affects reading and writing skills. However, this does not only affect these skills. Dyslexia is actually about processing information. People with dyslexia may have difficulty processing and remembering information they see and hear, which can affect learning and acquiring literacy skills. Dyslexia can also affect other areas such as organisational skills.

It is important to remember that there are positives in thinking differently. Many people with dyslexia display strengths in areas such as reasoning and in visual and creative areas.

Dyslexia is a disorder of the ability or even inability to read and comprehend. They may read a word correctly, but if they see it on the next page, they may not recognise it at all. They may not connect the written and spoken form of a word. Today, it is estimated that 1 in 10 people have dyslexia. This does not mean that they are not intelligent, on the contrary, they can be very successful academically in a number of fields. For many children with dyslexia, however, this fact is a source of low self-esteem and uncertainty about academic success, which can hinder their motivation. Therefore, such children need additional support and clarification of the specifics of their problem. It is often a matter of finding the right learning methods and strategies to help them overcome their problems.

This means that the teacher, when preparing their lessons, must take into account this diversity, because it is associated with specific difficulties in learning. It is imperative that the teacher assimilates the material and controls the behaviour of all these different adolescents. Exam preparation for any one of them can be more overwhelming and stressful than climbing a mountain. Transcribing text for them can also be a challenge.

They find it difficult to concentrate when reading or doing homework. They write slowly and therefore do not always finish tests and exams in the allotted time. They worry a lot about learning and avoid it as much as possible. They have problems at school because they tend not to listen or fall behind. Therefore, it is especially important to have adults by their side who will encourage and motivate them to see themselves as a big picture, and not just as one detail of it.

Dyslexia can have the same symptoms as farsightedness and near-sightedness, where without the help of glasses with the correct dioptres, the picture is blurred and unclear. This makes them insecure, and they feel afraid of everything related to learning and written text. For some kids, this turns out to be a convenient excuse to do nothing at school. They have difficulty concentrating and this is also similar to another diagnosis that is associated with attention deficit hyperactivity disorder, with the inability to focus on one thing for a long time. They are usually distracted, inattentive, restless, impulsive, and disorganised. That is why it is important, in case of doubts on the part of parents or teachers, that the child is tested in order to know in what direction the help is being given to them. Exam preparation will take more time. They will avoid reading books, so you have to find a way to get them to read what is enjoyable and interesting, not necessarily, you have to start somewhere. Reading and writing should not be associated with performance speed, as this may stress them out and they may refuse to do it. Pairing the audio of the same book can help make the reading experience more confident and interesting. Often, children with dyslexia learn the material more easily if there is someone next to them who, instead of making them read it, explains it to them themselves.

Unfortunately, in a school in a standard class, the teacher often has about thirty students and does not always have the opportunity to give individual attention to each one. Therefore, it is important that parents get involved and participate in the learning process of their child. Audiobooks combined with explanatory videos on 'YouTube' or other platforms can reduce their anxiety level and help them feel more confident that they too understand the instructions and information. The atmosphere of the learning environment is also important, it should be calm and inspiring. Therefore, they should have their own place where they can relax and stop worrying that others are watching how they are doing. In the exams themselves, children with dyslexia are often given more time to work on the exam tasks and are often allowed to use a computer device to record their answers.

Exam preparation itself can be organised in peer groups, where they will help each other. These are often their friends who are aware of their problems and accept them with understanding. Thus, they will combine work with pleasant company, and preparing for the exam will not feel like a punishment. Therefore, it is especially important that children are encouraged for their small successes and regularly reminded that those few small technical practical difficulties they experience in the learning process have nothing to do with their intelligence and how smart they are. Every child with dyslexia has an area and subject of study that they like, one that is easy for them and makes them happy. It is necessary to develop these areas, and not to emphasise those with which it does not cope. After all, a professional career can be developed in any field of human knowledge.

Now imagine that in this colourful classroom, which is full of teenagers with different problems, but also with problems that stem from their age, there are also bilingual children and their personal dramas and victories. A teacher must really be something of a magician to be able to handle all this variety.

Bilingual children are children who are born in a bilingual situation. This affects the families of immigrants who, for various reasons, find themselves on the territory of another country. Children in such families are forced to learn the larger, official language of the majority in whose country they are in order to be understood. This enables them to fit into school and work environments. On the other hand, each of these children in a similar situation has another home language in their family, which usually has limited functions and is used only between people who know this language.

In typical bilingualism, children usually have no difficulty with the official language of the country in which they study, because they were born in that country or come into it from a very young age. In such cases, they usually absorb the language easily and quickly, and it becomes their first language. This is because everyday conversations in this language crowd out the home language, whose functions may become stunted or not used for a long time. Comprehension problems usually occur when children enter a foreign language environment at middle school age. They then have real difficulty fitting into the classroom, which is buzzing with the official language. They need more time to learn the language and start using it quickly and effectively to achieve academic results. At the beginning, such children are very quiet, they feel lonely because no one understands them, and they do not understand anyone either. This can also be an obstacle to forming friendships.

Although at this age, adolescents are curious and open to each other. The boundaries of the groups they form are not impassable and they can also admit external classmates into these groups. They may even be quite supportive and sympathise with their classmate's situation. In this case, it will be easier for them to start using the new language, because emotionally they feel accepted by others. Unfortunately, however, there are also a number of cases when adolescents do not accept newcomers who do not yet speak their language, and this has a bad effect on their adaptation. These are cases of racism, competition, aggression, and others that prevent local children from opening up to newly arrived children from abroad. Very often, families also play a negative role here, in which prejudices and stereotypes about people are reflected in the conversations between adults and their children about emigrants.

More than how the other children behave in school towards each other, one can guess what the climate and mood is towards the foreign children in the families of their classmates. Children usually repeat their parents' words and share their views, sometimes full of prejudice and xenophobia.

Initially, such children need language help, at least in the beginning, until they can cope and understand the learning material on their own. Their difficulties are not only linguistic, but also related to their cultural identity, which finds itself in a new cultural environment and is forced to survive, adapt, and expand. For some children, this is a painful process associated with parting with old friends, with losses of emotional stability that they received from their old place of living and their old habits.

They have to start building their lives from scratch, in a new place and with new people, who sometimes have a bad attitude towards them. This can cause various personal crises in adolescence, in which the feeling of loneliness and isolation can lead to depression and an unwillingness to be a part of it all, which can be a step towards running back through memories, but also in reality. All this makes the classroom look like a beehive, in which everything is buzzing, and it is buzzing in its own way. All this variety can be a real challenge for a young teacher and for their students.

CONFLICTS BETWEEN GENERATIONS

In the adult world, everything may appear calm on the surface. Children view adults as people who can control themselves well, who always do the right thing, who make the right decisions, who are conscientious, responsible, kind, caring and rarely lose control. For children, adults are like angels, who have a halo over their heads. If we have to be honest, this is the image that adults project into the heads of their children in order to be able to control them better. Well, everything is about control and who will control whom. Adults want children not to make the mistakes they did when they were younger, and so they try to protect them, sometimes at all costs. Sometimes their determination to protect them exceeds a healthy understanding of caring, it can look and sound cruel and frightening.

Bad choices can affect what kind of friends children choose and what influence they have on them, how they spend their day, how much time they spend studying and how much for fun, how ambitious they are, and a host of other things. The desire of parents to protect their children from wrong steps is completely understandable and acceptable because they, from their position as people with greater social and life experience, know what the consequences can be. They know that the missed years are difficult to catch up on, and they understand that it is not easy to combine the high demands of academic success, the work and discipline that come with this. Some adults may even remember how difficult it was for them. In fact, the paradox is that adults may remember when they were children, but due to the rules and prohibitions placed by society, there have been changes and transformations in their understanding.

We often hear adults awaiting their 'Friday night', which are reflections of the desire adults have to escape from society and their obligations to it. It is a sign that in the world of adults, not everything is whole, harmonious, mature, and calm. Adhering to the philosophy that when we are at work we do not live, but only live when we are having 'fun', has a seriously traumatic effect on the psyche of working adults. This philosophy makes us perceive our life as fragmented and with resistance to anything that is not related to the ideology of fun and rest. Due to this notion, adults may perceive work as a route which provokes stress and rejection. Adults pass on their fragmented philosophy of life to their children, and then they are surprised that children also resist everything related to school, learning, work, or discipline. The philosophy that our life consists of separate pieces, events happening in separate places and seemingly unrelated to each other, can only provoke stress and an unwillingness to be a part of it. A huge contradiction on the part of adults.

Sometimes adults encourage children to do things, they may themselves not do. Adults tend to emphasise that whilst being at work, they are not 'living'. Children mimic these tones and apply it to their 'work' setting, which for them is their school. Children are like sponges, they absorb information and mirror the actions of adults. However, adults should encourage children to perceive their life as a whole and to love everything they do, because this is how they will realise all the opportunities the world has to offer. However, if they continuously hear and observe stressed adults at work, then this will distort the positive position in their mindset.

Conflicts are inherent in the way adults choose to raise their children. They must be fair to both parties. However, it often turns out that there are super high standards, demands and expectations for children that must compensate for the failures of their parents. The problem is often not even the expectations, but the way in which those expectations are controlled. The problem is in the overcontrol that adults exert, in the methods of influence and education.

What kind of adults do teenagers see around them? Are they loving, helpful, sympathetic, joyful, present, and friendly? Or are the adults they see more controlling, forbidding, criticising, selfish, self-obsessed, indifferent, absent-minded, and lazy? Adults with their views and actions are the mirror that children reflect for themselves. Well, at least it was before they hit puberty. This is where adults find it difficult to manage their emotions, as they want children to be under their control and to obey their every command. However, when transitioning, it is difficult for children to remain in these boxes. They will test the boundaries and explore what they feel is 'right'. Due to children seeking this independence, adults feel personally neglected and affected by this fact. At times, it is over-controlling adults who cause trouble for teenagers.

One of the main causes of intergenerational conflicts is that adults prefer to communicate with adolescents from the position of their functions, the role they have in the family or at school. These are, in most cases, authoritarian functions and roles. At the same time, exercising their divine functions, they believe that they themselves are absolutely infallible in everything. For example, for some children, their parent or caregiver is an absolute hero. They are perceived as an outright deity, one who has absolute authority in everything. When children transition into teenagers, their view of their parents or caregivers being a 'hero' begins to change.

This creates a paradox. Driven by their nature, children continue to change, but their parents refuse to leave their 'divine throne'. It can be very easy to be a deity, some adults may resort to negative methods to assert their authority. Young children fall for these divine tricks, as they do not yet have social experience and in this sense are naive. Teenagers like to check their own experiences out, which can often lead to conflicts with the adults in their world, which tends to be a popular mode of communication at this stage. Why do adults refuse to change? Is it because they are tired of society, they think they know everything and so do not care? Adults want it easy. How can you blame them? With teenagers it is not easy and if the adults do not choose to change the relationship, they are doomed. In order for there to be no conflicts and for communication to be relatively problem-free, mutual compromise and negotiation is required. We want both sides to be perceived as equals. Adults must learn to communicate with children as equals, and as friends, as they do with their own friends. It is important to create a world with democracy, moderate liberalism combined with negotiable frameworks and rules. A friendly atmosphere, one which is moderate, with healthy selfishness, a mutual discovery of each other's world, joy in being altruistic and attempts to like them, combined with empathy.

Problems tend to come from adults continuing to behave like functions rather than people. For some adults such as parents, caregivers or teachers may find it shocking to hear that children should see them in any form of vulnerability. If this transformation happens with the adult, then problems may be greatly reduced. Authoritarianism, violence, the desire to impose oneself at all costs, causing unhappiness to one's own child, destructive criticism, over-control, the desire to own, humiliation, cruelty to assert one's ego through the absolute obedience of the child, are all acts that are set to destroy any glimmer of love. They similarly mimic a relationship between a perpetrator and victim, a master, and their slave, with relationships of compassion and love being absent.

Constant conflicts lead to harassment of the adolescent at home and contributes to the unwillingness to be a part of their family. This is because their family may make them feel unhappy, misunderstood, and often they are afraid of their parents and their desire to escape from this place is often realised. Children then look for people outside the family who will listen to them, who will understand them, who will pay attention to them as individuals, and who will perceive them as equals. This way of communicating will create trust between the two parties, in which neither wants to impose their own opinion and control.

The main conflicts between generations are similar to evolutionary times, and if often for territory, food, influence, dominance, boundaries and for control. This stems from our similar biological nature. Unfortunately, both within the family and in their school environment, they uncover the most amount of criticism they will ever face at this age.

Adults are not conversing and communicating with still paintings in an art gallery but are communicating with adolescents who have a wide array of emotions, heightened by their distrust of society and at times the adults around them. Survival as an adult is different in a world like this. Adolescents are mobile and watch for the slightest opportunity to knock you, the adult, off the pedestal. Almost like in the jungle, where they have a master authority that they obey and often they want to please more than you. It is not easy to be both cool and strict at the same time, to follow the traditions of society, but also to be a free thinker. Teenagers will test this ability in you, constantly. If you go into communication with them with the idea that you are going to a war and that you must win, then you can be sure to lose the war, as your rationale for communicating is toxic. Moreover, you are approaching from the position of the authoritarian tyrant, from authority, control, and rules. Eventually, they will approach unconventionally, creatively, inventing new rules, tactics, and strategies with which in turn will cause an adult's defeat. Not only that, they will laugh at you afterwards and will consider you as a weak and predictable adult, who is somehow rigid and conservative, and unaccustomed to free thinking.

We must remember that we are communicating with the soul, thoughts, and emotions of children. As adults, we must show respect, delicacy, acceptance and liking. We have to be able to compromise and to accept the point of view of the opposition of the children.

UPBRINGING, NOT TRAINING AND TAMING

Upbringing and education are familiar constructs which most individuals are familiar with. It is difficult to convince a person who follows authoritarian methods, that humane methods are actually the ones that win the heart of the audience. It is the humane methods that can make someone soar after meeting us and vice versa. Authoritarian methods often suggest that we are incapable, inferior and that we are not good enough. With authoritarian methods, you can achieve military-type discipline and obedience, but this will be achieved from fear and sense of self-preservation.

There is an important difference between making a human being suitable to fit the demands of society and making an animal fit into human society. The differences are huge, and they arise mostly from the specifics of the two biological species – humans and animals. However, the differences are also the result of the limitations and opportunities that humans and animals have. We mean mostly intellectual and mental abilities. To make a dog fit into human society, you need to train it to respond to certain commands, for the dog to sit, stand up, be quiet, etc. Some types of dogs, for example, are so intelligent that they can be trained to rescue people, detect drugs and more. It takes some time to train a dog to do this. Also proverbial is the dog's loyalty, the joy, and the emotions of affection that a dog shows towards its owner. They are able to remember for a long time the smell of people who are good and kind to them and happily wag their tails, and also jump for joy, waiting for a pat and a hug. This is a sign that people also remember them and respond to these emotions, and often dogs are regarded as a man's best friend. The methods used to train the dog are a combination of authoritarian commands that, with their consistency, create patterns of behaviour in the dog. Repeated often, they become part of the animal's emotional and physical memory.

Of course, in the training process, humans show both affection and joy towards the dog, which actually makes the emotional bond between the two species possible. Mutual love, mutual joy, companionship, and mutual help are something that is valued by humans and dogs alike. Both species express this in their own unique way, but at the same time in a very similar way.

Stroking, hugging, kissing, rewarding, and going for a walk, are all ways to show our love for the animal. Unfortunately, there are still people who are cruel to animals, including dogs. They may beat them, kick them, push them, starve them, sell them and a bunch of other horrible scenarios that human fantasy and cruelty are unfortunately capable of giving birth to. Animals unfortunately cannot communicate against the horrors that they are experiencing and often suffer in silence. Dogs sometimes communicate with their eyes when they are sad, but often hold on to the moment where they may receive some form of affection or a 'petting', where all is forgiven.

If a human behaves this way towards animals, then how must they treat their children? Is there really no difference? This is the big question to which humane pedagogy seeks and offers answers. What do we do with children in the process of education and training? What methods do we use to avoid the risk of turning relationships with children into a process of domestication and taming? We often try to train and tame them, applying the same methods as we do with animals.

But children can talk. They can protest. They may disagree. They can also scream. They can also sometimes physically assault adults. By our own actions, we are nurturing and visibly training children to act as aggressive bullies using the same authoritarian methods that we apply towards them. How do we break this vicious cycle of reproduction of authoritarianism? Remember, adults are the mirror through which children see the new world they are entering. They come onto this planet and may come across some angry creatures screaming with twisted faces, waving fists, shooting words and some who strike children. Then they wonder where this aggression in children comes from, and why some children are so cruel and ungrateful. Well, children learn these methods from adults, this is what they see in their family and at school. This is the picture of the world that adults paint in front of children, and not with their words, but with their daily behaviour and actions. Like is brought up by like.

If small children can resemble small puppies in some ways, even if they try to bite you sometimes, they generally fear and trust adults. However, this is not always the case with teenagers. We agree that upbringing is about limiting, setting social frameworks, and following rules, but how these rules are implemented is important. Yelling, screaming, criticism, manipulation, threats, and punishments may not be the best way to instil positive values. Perhaps with love, creative patience, negotiation, mutual respect, and equal dialogue it can be achieved. A person is a very complex combination of expressions of energy, intellectual, spiritual, psychic, and emotional systems. Our ability to understand ourselves and the processes that happen to us, our ability to produce thoughts and ideas that become products, all initiates an understanding of what lies behind the limited and mortal matter of the material. It can even turn us into spiritual adventure seekers.

Our ability to consciously express positive and negative emotions and direct them to the object of our feelings, but also to be able to read their emotional signals, makes us beings capable of reaching out for help as well as hurting. This is the huge difference between us and the rest of the living beings on the planet, as animals and plants simply follow their life cycle set for them by nature. We can consciously decide to break this cycle and choose another path. It is an ability that is a result of the development of our consciousness as well. It is the adult's conscious choice to stop taming and training children, as they usually do this with animals. That is the turning point that must occur in any adult, parent, caregiver or teacher. We do not just issue commands and they just follow them. This, for such a complex biological being as a human, is no longer enough, and is often humiliating. There is no child or adult who will be satisfied only with this type of relationship, one full of commands, instructions, and obedience. We carry within us a more developed consciousness and worldview in which our roles occur on an equal, respectful, and spiritual basis.

We suffer when they only treat us with commands, which means they do not respect our right to an opinion, our right to vote, or our right to disapprove of it. When we are forbidden to speak on the matter, we simply lose interest and look for another environment that will be more healthy, harmonious, and equal. We are looking for an environment where we will be considered interesting, which will devote time and attention to us, and which will value us.

That is exactly what teenagers do. Today's teenagers are the children of the creators of artificial intelligence and all these magical technologies that we use. They carry within them an aspiration for space flight. Only with training and taming, something so primitive and ordinary as methods, yet it just does not work with them. Children in today's society are born informed and smart and they expect to see such adults around them. They are born with a spiritual hunger and expect to see adults who will offer them spiritual food. What do they often see? Primitive methods that degrade relationships to the level of master and slave. This is humiliating for today's teenagers. They can find a bunch of information, academic studies, and facts in a second, with which they will use to prove to you the harm adults can cause from using authoritarian methods. They will even find laws that can bring you under legal responsibility, while you helplessly blink your eyes and wonder how you never protested when your authoritarian parents trained you and you obediently agreed, because you were afraid. Do you think that your children and students must also fear you and obey your commands blindly without comment or discussion? Today's teenagers are different, they are freer, more capable, more combinatory, and arguably are the children of the creators of new 'magical' technologies. In fact, the humiliation is for us adults who cannot and do not succeed in following the growth of human consciousness. Being authoritarian is easier. To choose intelligent, dignified, and respectful methods is an act of conscious choice and means that you perceive yourself as a free intelligent and spiritual being who is not afraid of competition and disobedience, but consciously wants to participate in the collective education and spiritual training of others. This is because children do not belong to us. They come from the cosmos as bits of energy, which in order to become visible pass through us to take visible form. Often adults can make this divine energy miserable.

In purely practical terms, within our daily lives,

adults must teach children how to create rules that are fair, just, and socially acceptable to all. This is only possible if adults change their attitude within themselves towards adolescents, who they perceive as a category of people who are of low value and only have to listen and have no say in anything. Such an approach to them will one day backfire on adults, because they reflect what they see in us.

Therefore, the education of adolescents must be based on mutual respect, which comes not only from them to adults, but also in the opposite direction. They need to see people who listen to their opinions and who take an interest in their lives as they are, not as we wish them to be. This means that the dialogue between us is of particular importance. If they do not like some of our rules, then a communication point should be established between children and adults. It is also imperative to be open to any criticism the child may have towards you and to discuss a way in which both parties can move forward positively. Discuss and if necessary, modify your initial plan to reflect their vision. For this, courageous and self-confident adults are needed who are ready to make compromises, and in this way, they will teach adolescents how to make compromises in such conflict and crisis situations. Equal cooperation, persuasion, but not management. Order and harmony in society is based on the negotiation of rules and compromises.

As mentioned earlier, a paradox occurs. Children today, following the impulses laid in them by cosmic intelligence, do not simply follow the processes of development, but build on it. They meet adults who consciously resist these processes, resist the progress and development laid down by nature, because they fear losing the control on which their illusory greatness is built. Our methods of education and upbringing lag behind the development of the energies that children carry, as representatives not only of the human species, but also of the great cosmic intelligence. In this sense, evolution for us is not only biological, but also spiritual, evolution of human consciousness.

Upbringing and education is a process of creating masterpieces, where the processes are mutual and come down to the following principles: love, understanding, acceptance and forgiveness.

YOU ARE A UNIQUE PHENOMENON AND I ADMIRE YOU

A positive vision of the world and the people around us is a reflection of our own loftiness and nobility. Our own assessment, belief, and decision to see and discover the positive sides of what surrounds us reflects ourselves, it is the mirror through which we can look into a person's soul. The ability to see the beauty in others is also a result of our inner desire and attitude to create beauty around us. This includes human relationships. After meeting others, people should feel elevated, left with a better opinion and impressions, not just for us, but for themselves. Our words, actions and gestures should make others believe that they are that miracle whose meeting and conversation we have been waiting for a long time. A miracle that changes us too. Such a benevolent attitude and faith are also the basis of upbringing and education. It has even more to do with how we see teenagers and what words we use to convey those impressions. Our words can uplift and make a teenager fly, but they can also have the opposite effect. Words that are full of criticism, pessimism, disapproval, misunderstanding and non-acceptance can break the weak wings of an adolescent for a long time. They can damage not only your relationships, but also a teenager's own self-esteem, which is still so fragile. Positive words can make them see the world and life as an opportunity and an adventure in which they are the heroes whose appearance the world has been waiting for. A world where their talents, alongside their overall appearance of a dignified being, can contribute to progress and positive changes in the world. On the contrary, the negative words that adults say to a teenager can make them feel worthless, and full of self-doubt, which will result from the constant criticism and disapproval that comes from adults.

This is why it is so important to paint teenagers with bright, positive colours and words that reflect that vision. It is the result of realising our own responsibility to raise and educate worthy people. The source of this faith and hope of ours in adolescents must be found within the hearts of adults.

Painting with positive words is a magical method that stems from our desire to actively create good. There is nothing greater than lifting someone up, raising someone's self-esteem, telling them that they are kind, good, invaluable, and indispensable. Every adult, when communicating with adolescents, is obliged to elevate, but not humiliate adolescents. This method helps to emphasise qualities, and also suggests those that are still missing, but with our help and faith, they will develop. This is especially important for adolescents, who may be confused, insecure, timid, shy, depressed, protesting, idealistic, and confident that the world begins with them. These energies can and should be channelled in the right direction, so that they are not dispersed and lost, but hold a positive vision for themselves and for the world around us is built over them.

Which qualities of adolescents should be emphasised and developed? There are so many, yet there are some bright and pure energies without which life would be an unbearable place to live. The meaning of upbringing and education is in exaltation, not in humiliation. This is the path to mutual spiritual growth, of the adult and the adolescent. Only spiritually elevated individuals can build a world without violence against the personality of adolescents. To achieve this big goal, we need to do something very small every day. You need constant friendly communication with teenagers, listening without judging and criticising, just be there for them to be a part of their life. It is that simple. This is how they will begin to perceive themselves as people who are interesting and important interlocutors. They have the right to make mistakes and experience negative emotions. They are still learning to understand why things happen to them, so it is important for them to be able to express the emotions that events in their lives evoke in them. During this process, they should know that adults will not judge them for their mistakes but will try to help them so that they can develop a sense of responsibility. Only unconditional love and acceptance are capable of gently and humanely correcting some behavioural errors. The adolescent needs to support themselves in the process of their personal crises and dramas, when friends abandon and leave them, and they may feel as though the whole world is against them. It is important for them to understand that you, as the adults, will always be there for them. In such situations, the adult must connect with the adolescent's emotions, trying to understand them, and responding with sympathy. The teenager needs to hear that their thoughts, feelings, and emotions are important to the adult, and that they need to feel your love. At the centre of their relationship there should be love, care, respect, and mutual admiration.

Therefore, when the adolescent is in a moment of crisis and disappointment, adults should paint their next bright moment, so that they have the strength to cope with the momentary weakness and fight.

Certain qualities, sensations and states are able to make us feel special, festive, and extraordinary. They should be developed in adolescents with the help of painting with positive words.

Nobility. Magnanimity

Adults must learn to show nobility and magnanimity in their dealings with adolescents in order to teach them how to recognise these two fine qualities. In relationships, it often happens that we show pettiness, have a bad memory, prefer to remember only the small unpleasant details, to remind them endlessly. This can be exhausting and poisonous to any relationship. When adults are supposed to model their behaviour and words for teenagers, such behaviour then becomes a bad example that teens not only learn from, they simply copy to win their battles with adults. We all make mistakes, both adults and teenagers. It is pointless to keep reminding them when their impact has long passed, and they no longer matter.

Adults like to bring up past failures and mistakes as if they control the situation by instilling feelings of guilt and shame. Sometimes it seems to us that being bad-mouthed, preferring to remember only bad deeds, is like showing how good we really are and how wrong others are. Having a bad memory is a kind of punishment that backfires on us like a boomerang. The backlash is similar, and an ugly game of verbal ping pong begins, with no winners, only hurt.

The opposite of malice is magnanimity and nobility of character. It is magnanimous for an adult to give in, understand and forgive. There are so many positive occasions and actions that adults should use to encourage and empower, not wear down and humiliate teenagers. Therefore, positive actions should be exaggerated and emphasised, especially at times when the adolescent is filled with disbelief, lack of self-confidence and feeling as though their whole world is collapsing. It is at such moments that adults should take the paint brush, dip it in the most beautiful positive paints and paint a picture of success, of courage, of victories for the adolescent with words. Only in this way will the adolescent learn how to support other people in similar situations. They must not only have seen this from the elders, but they must have experienced for themselves the beneficial and healing effect of nobility and magnanimity painted in positive words and deeds. Paint with positive words nobility and magnanimity. Accept your differences and forgive each other.

Admiration

Admiration and inspiration go hand in hand.

Communication between adults and adolescents should be based on mutual admiration, which should be a source of constant inspiration for communication. It should be built on the basis of mutual respect, appreciation, and enjoyment of communication. These feelings of positive appreciation of each other's personality can turn into mutual creative inspiration. Admiration of the other happens when we see the other as special, exceptional, unique and when we emphasise these qualities.

Mutual admiration should become a beautiful habit that is practically similar to painting with positive words and exchanging compliments, becoming a ritual of your daily life where you are focused on seeing and developing the positive. As for the negative manifestations, they are calmly analysed, and a lesson is learned from them. Inspiration in communication between adults and adolescents can also be perceived as communication with joy, with mutual interest, when each learns something from the other and feels validated for his successes. By their own example, adults should set an example for teens of what admiration is, using any occasion to admire something the teen has accomplished. Any progress should be encouraged and encouraged with words, a smile, an approving pat on the shoulder, a hug when appropriate. Thus, adolescents will learn that they are valuable, unique, special, and most importantly valued and noticed by adults. Only in this way will they learn how to practice and use the power of admiration and spread the healing energy around them in various situations they may find themselves in. A relationship that is based on mutual admiration that comes from soul energies, and it is an immortal relationship because it vibrates at a level that is elevated above the material. Conversely, a relationship that is based only on admiration of the body, is a relationship that is limited, because that is the nature of matter and the physical. It is limited and short-lived. Paint boldly the colours of admiration and inspiration.

Patience

Patience is a virtue that every adult should develop in dealing with teenagers. At school or at home, the adult must arm themselves with a lot of patience to help the adolescent go through this transitional period and keep their relationships at a high and beautiful level. Patience is needed when they are hysterical, when they reject you, when they think you can no longer be their authority, when they are reaching out into the big world and when you are no longer enough for them. Even more patience is needed when they even shout at you, when they fall into bad company and pick up bad habits that are hard to give up. Patience is needed when they deny you, although you need to be patient even if you feel your heart is broken to pieces. Patience is needed when they humiliate you in front of the whole class to prove that they too have the right to be brave. This is when you should show magnanimity and be patient like an angel because you know that all of this is temporary and will pass, but they do not know that. They are in the hot cauldron of their emotions as everything inside them rages and destroys. Only active, creative patience can help to get through these crisis trials. This is a state in which the adult not only waits for the storm to pass, but continues to build the relationship, giving it a chance and forgiving. This is the only way you will teach them how to be patient, how to wait and not to rush their decisions and not to throw strong words in a dramatic moment. It is important to take a deep breath and consider what the consequences of the said words will be for them. Paint patience in teenagers, but first paint it in yourself. You will need tons of patience in communicating with teenagers. Active, creative patience, filled with love.

Trust

Trust is like a delicate invisible web that is hard to build but very easy to tear. Without mutual trust, relationships are impossible. Here the adult must be especially careful in what they do, say and the tone in how they communicate. Trust is associated with faith, mercy, confidence, conviction, sincerity, respect, and help. Trust is the realisation that someone can count on you, no matter what happens, under any circumstances and it is like a connecting thread between two people. When you trust someone, you can tell them personal and intimate things about yourself, and you know that they will not share this with others. They will respect your desire for discretion and delicacy. When you trust someone, you are not afraid to share your mistakes with them, because you are sure that they will not criticise you but will understand you and find words to encourage you.

What kills trust? Lying, breaking promises, betrayal, constant criticism, negativity, a strong desire to control another person's secrets and mistakes, can all result in a shutdown of trust. When you act more in your own interest than in the interest of the person who trusted you. All this is also important for relationships between adults and adolescents, who especially need a trusted person. They need a person who will listen to them, try to understand them, comfort them, and find a way to help them if necessary. The trusted person will not constantly criticise them, focusing only on their mistakes.

This is why it is so important at home and at school that teenagers see in the face of older people whom they can trust, particularly in difficult moments.

People for whom teenagers are more important than the rules they make. If adolescents cannot find trusting adults at home or at school, they will try to find them outside that circle. Unfortunately, they sometimes fall prey to people who take advantage of their naivety and inexperience. This is why adults need to paint with positive words and build upon the components of trust with adolescents. Adults need to work on themselves and clean up or suppress all their negative sides that can destroy trust and tear that invisible web that connects them and adolescents.

Compassion

Compassion is a state in which we, with our hearts, are able to feel someone else's pain. Compassion is associated with sympathy, pity, mutual understanding and empathising with someone else's emotion. It is the acceptance of the other person as an equal being. It is a desire to free other people from their suffering. It is based on respect for the difficulties they have gone through and the desire to help them. The easiest way to feel someone else's pain is to put ourselves in their shoes and in their situation to feel and understand. Without compassion and mutual aid, the human world would be a cold and cruel place.

The energies of love and compassion are the main

spiritual food without which spiritual growth is impossible. Without them, the survival of humans as a species is impossible. Kindness is the active ingredient of compassion; it gives action and makes things happen. Showing kindness is our liberation from the selfish prison in which we lock ourselves. It is the door through which our heart meets another heart to free it from anxiety and loneliness.

Compassion makes us happier and more confident, filling us with reassurance that we have something to give to other people. The positive thing about compassion is that its supply is endless and impossible to exhaust. This makes us humans rich. Compassion must be developed. Every human being is capable of acts of compassion and adults have a duty to raise generations who are able to feel someone else's pain and provide comfort to ease it. In order for adolescents to develop compassion, they need to see adults around them who practice kindness towards other people. Adults should approach adolescents' problems with respect and show sympathy and compassion. No matter how small or large these problems are, they deserve your respect. Only in this way will you teach adolescents to show respect for yourself in situations where you need compassion. If you approach adolescent problems with disbelief and derision and do not recognise them as real problems, because of the children's age, then do not expect compassion from them when you are in trouble. Like is bred by like.

So, paint with positive words, display your sympathy and desire to help, because sympathy must be active to have an effect. Show your unreserved support to teens. Paint your devotion and love in a way that leaves no doubt that you are on their side, no matter what happens and no matter what they do. You will support them in the difficult path of correcting their wrong doings. This is a sure way to create a unique relationship in which spiritual growth will be a magical adventure for all of you. You deserve to rise above mortal matter and connect with the energies that come from the heart. This will ensure immortality of your spirit and soul. Teenagers will follow you on this unique journey.

Repentance. Forgiveness

Remorse is a state of regret for our actions. It is the feeling of guilt when you have done wrong, or when you have said words that hurt. It also relates to making a decision to change the way of life or thinking that may have led to the wrong actions or words. It is a complete rethinking and a desire to atone for the guilt. Repentance is associated with asking for forgiveness, which is a sign of acknowledging wrongdoing. It is an outstretched hand, and an attempt to build a bridge. In moral terms, for the spiritual growth of a person, repentance is extremely important. It is the medicine that heals the wounds inflicted on the soul and the heart. In this case, words are used that express our regret, words full of love and a promise that this will not happen again. Remorse and apologies are the way to keep trust between us. They show that it is important for us that our relationships develop joyfully, respectfully, and equally.

As adults, we often stare at the mistakes of teenagers, which we observe under a magnifying glass and constantly remind them of. We insist that teenagers apologise to us for every wrong step, yet how often do teenagers hear from adults the words of a sincere apology for their mistakes? Is it because adults are sinless and have protection from a special law? If adults have never apologised to their children, then they should start considering doing so. This enables them to show to adolescents that they too can make mistakes and consider themselves as equals to them.

The process of apologising should not go in a direction where the one apologising humiliates themselves. Humiliation has no place in upbringing and education. An apology is showing respect for the other, and it is respect for their honour and dignity. Teenagers deserve an apology for the authoritarian methods you may treat them with, as they are not wild animals that are to be trained mercilessly. No, they are thinkers, who are intelligent and equal human beings with free will. If they have been wronged, then they deserve a sincere apology. Therefore, grab the brush and with positive words paint the portrait of their uniqueness. Accept. Understand. Forgive. Love.

CONSCIOUS EXPANSION OF IDENTITY BOUNDARIES

The ability to change and adapt to a changing environment is critical to our survival as a species. Historically, this change has affected both the physical development of the human body, albeit at a slower pace and less pronounced visible changes, and changes in how the mental and intellectual processes in humans take place. The changes in how we see the world around us and within us has led to many qualitative changes in our view of the bigger picture of the world; a small energetic part of which we co-exist individually. This means that the biological and spiritual evolution of humans as a species, is laid down by a higher power that we do not control, but whose impulses we feel as the driving force of our life processes. This makes us part of the bigger picture of the cosmos. A number of studies show that there is an incredible visual similarity between the picture of the structure of the human brain, for example, and the structure of the cosmos.

Another major similarity with other living biological species is that our human lives also consist of life cycles that we do not choose, but simply follow. Some of them are related to growth and aging, reproduction, the need for food and some others that affect our biological survival. A huge advantage to the survival of humans as a species, however, turns out to be the advantage given to us by our magnificent brain and its abilities. This is a result of millions of years of evolution. The brain is associated with intellect, which is a powerful tool in our efforts to survive. In addition to an amazing brain, humans also possess a complexity of tools that are capable of helping us change the direction of the cyclicality embedded in us by nature. We can choose to eat or not, to reproduce or not. Our every action and thought can be the result of a conscious choice, which shows the power of the human will, as a way of self-control to choose and change. It is such a wealth of possibilities.

The ability to control our own thoughts and emotions, may be the most natural thing for people of the 21st century? Actually, this is the most difficult thing, to control the thoughts and the emotions that follow after them, many research papers say that the thought comes first and then the emotion echoes. Sometimes the emotion is so strong that it takes a long time to disappear. It seems easier to say: "You made me unhappy", than to admit to yourself that you did not actually do anything to make yourself feel less sad. Everything happens inside of us, and the people outside are just the stimuli; the impulses to trigger our own capacities to feel sadness, pain, joy or even love. It is somehow easier and more profitable, because of our desire to emotionally manipulate others, to melodramatically state that it is others' fault and that we are unhappy.

It turns out that adults who master this powerful self-control of thought and emotion should be simply great wizards in the process of upbringing and education. Why do we keep going around in cycles of our own mistakes and instead of consciously choosing to stop making the same wrong choices, we automatically do the same things over and over again? If conscious actions and thoughts are so difficult of a choice for adults, then why do we insist that children must master the self-control of their thoughts and emotions to perfection? Why is there a consideration to punish them afterwards, if they express an emotion which we do not like? How ignorant and hypocritical the adult world is.

Mindfulness is the ability to live in the present

moment without judgement and be 100% present in it, as well as letting go of automatic patterns of behaviours, thoughts, and emotions. This is what adults must achieve for themselves first, so that they can then help adolescents by showing them healthy, adequate, and correct images and patterns of behaviour. However, this means that adults must constantly change. To change the ways in which they respond, to change their absence in the adolescent's world and turn it into a presence, to change their indifference to conscious listening and attentiveness to what the child shares. Also, to change their own fears that make them domineering tyrants, capable only of criticising, grumbling, condemning by quick procedure, and disapproving.

Changing who we think we are is a painful process. Historically, in order not to lose themselves mentally and to achieve some kind of mental stability, children are told at an early age who and what they are. These are such labels that adults stick to children, with a 'special glue' that can never be removed. This is mostly because adults do not want to remove these tags, as it is easier for them to manipulate and educate something that does not move, change, yet just stands there motionless and politely listens to you with adoration.

However, reality is far from this fantasy. In reality, all living things are constantly changing. Change is the only option for living things. The weather, the climate, celestial phenomena change, and plants all go through their life cycles. Animals are increasingly amenable to training and domestication, and their ability to respond adequately emotionally to humans is increasingly impressive in view of what hidden and unknown capacities for development and evolution they display within themselves. All living things change every second. The scenario may be that you may have gotten married yesterday and shared the eternal "I love you", but today has rolled around and suddenly you are not so sure anymore. Emotions change and catch us off guard, leaving us confused. This is because we cannot own someone else just by virtue of the fragile emotions that bind us together. Adults are the ones who should prepare children about these changes, which are normal, as they are part of changing life. Adults should also allow adolescents to change, not to be in constant opposition to these processes, but to support them and be part of the changes. This is why children should grow up without labels, and with the freedom that loving adults give them to change themselves. Freedom to evolve, to choose their own identity if they want it so much.

Often the adults are opposed to these changes, more out of the inertia of how they were raised than out of a lack of love for their children, although it often seems the other way around. The legacy that adults carry is not always joyful and positive and are often related to the use of authoritarian methods that their parents exercised on them. They automatically and unconsciously pass this on to their children and students as taught by the previous generation. As a result, a number of conflicts occur, because children today are different, and some children try to act in a much more conscious way than the adults who surround them. It turns out that children with development, overtake the methods and pedagogies of the past, with which adults do not want to part from. How does one change the habits, cyclical thinking, and actions of adults in order to obtain joyful communication with the new generation, and to improve relationships and the results of academic and educational processes? Only with a conscious change in adults of the qualities that interfere with the process of communication with adolescents. We must change to help them too to reflect more dignified images and patterns of behaviour. Self-control, not uncontrollable adult rights.

Identity is what we have been told we are, and we have remembered it. It is as if we stuck a label on our chest with our description, as is done with product descriptions. Identity is a set of characteristics and qualities, inclusive of social, cultural, ethnic, moral, religious, professional and many others. It is belonging to something, which results in a conscious choice of inherited and suggested choices by adults for children. Identity should not be something once and for all given and accepted, but in the process of changes, adaptations, and expansion. Only in this way can we develop and transform, and only in this way can we reflect the duality of our nature - energy and material.

Conscious identity expansion is particularly important for upbringing and education. This will make us more tolerant and willing to compromise in our interactions with adolescents, which in turn will avoid conflicts. It will give softness and friendliness to our character, which will allow us to accept with understanding the choices of our teenagers, realising that even their wrong choices are something temporary that can be changed in mutual respectful dialogue and compromises. If we listen to them and accept them as they are today, they will also hear and accept us as we are. Imperfect, but in a constant process of development.

Here we come up against something really very powerful - our habits accumulated over the years. Habits in our reactions, thoughts, way of speaking, criticising, and condemning, shouting, and adding to the mental pressure, even if there is no need for it. All these wrong habits of ours destroy the trust of teenagers in us, which will make them look for trusted individuals external to their home unit. Our habits gradually turn from comfort to our prison, which we consciously maintain, because we consciously perceive them as part of who we are, a part of our identity. There must be a way out of this fruitless circle. The way out for us as adults is whenever we see that something is not working and is not improving our relationships with our teenagers, then we need to stop. Stop, look at each other from the sides and with the eyes of the distance to give up the act that is no longer capable of being the bridge that connects us with our children. It becomes our frame, a cage from which there is no exit. Our spiritual development is impossible without the spiritual discipline that will help us take the step toward conscious effort and conscious choice against the habits and cyclicality that keep us only at a biological level of development. Only the biological level of development related to nutrition and reproduction benefit from repeating the same movements and choices because they ensure our survival and continuation as a species. Our energy essence suffers from a similar cyclicity, from which there is no development, but looping and degradation. The only way out of the cage of habits is to start breaking free from them, a little bit every day, fully consciously. Adopting conscious thoughts, words and actions as our philosophy will help us to stop moving in circles, stop seeing ourselves as just a product description label and gradually expand who we are energetically and spiritually.

The expansion of our identity is practically limitless and is the result of spiritual quests and transformations. Our identification must be with the entire cosmos, and from the standpoint of our thinking mind and feeling heart. This does not lead to a blurring of our energy boundaries, but on the contrary, to an increase in our power, energy strength and volume. Realising that you are also the bee that you stepped on on purpose a moment ago, that you are also the water in the river that you deliberately pollute, that you are also the majestic trees that you quite knowingly cut down to sell, will bring about changes in you yourself. Your awareness, responsibility, and care for everything around you will increase, because you will realise that this is care for yourself in the present and future moment. The realisation that you are also the person who intentionally crashed your car will lead to moral and ethical transformations in you about where the limits of what is permissible in society are. Can we kill and steal, or will it backfire on us for the simple reason that we are both the one we robbed and the one we killed? We are the common collective pain, joy, sorrow, but also compassion, mercy, and love.

Such adults will help the next generation choose love, peace, compassion, kindness, altruism, and humanity. Hatred, selfishness, and greed for the same biological needs, cyclically genetically transmitted from generation to generation and leading to wars, will gradually become a thing of the past. We would like to believe that adolescents will encounter more such adults both at home and at school, which should not be a place that pursues only pragmatic goals and results that can be expressed in percentages. The point of evolution is spiritual improvement, not just biological changes.

Having said this, it is a long road, on which we must first have the patience to plant the tree, to provide it with nutrients, for the bees to pollinate its flowers, and only after several years of constant care, perseverance, and patience, we may enjoy its fruits. The path from planting the tree to picking the apples is a path filled with active creative patience. The path of upbringing and education is similar. Being aware of the difficulties along the way makes us open to making conscious choices that will gradually change us, as adults, but also our teenagers. They will be provided with a calm and stimulating environment for living and development. An environment where intergenerational communication will occur with the blessing of the entire cosmic home, of which we are a part of. The path to spiritual growth will become a path full of joyful adventures, discoveries and transformations into our higher forms and essences.

THE CROOKED MIRRORS OF THE CONSUMER SOCIETY

Today we live in a time of material abundance. Compared to people a few centuries ago, today each of us has the same material comforts for living that only the very rich had in the past. This is a huge advance in improving the living conditions of most people. At the same time, it is also a huge waste of planet earth's resources. The abundance of matter also leads to the obsession with owning many things, as we are manipulated by the powerful weapon of business advertising, each of us is more or less partial to shopping. This, in turn, can lead adolescents to perceive life only from this side, the one of materialism, following the power of money. The danger of such a consumptive view of life is that it can lead to spiritual blindness and stunting the ability and desire to seek something more, which is beyond the perishable limitations of matter.

By making short-term profits, businesses are harming the upbringing and education of children today. Quite deliberately, the business uses advertising as a weapon with which it insinuates, manipulates, misinforms the people who, for the business, are in the role of consumers and customers. Children and young people are the most affected by deliberate business misinformation. It is precisely those whom we expect in the future to show common sense, reasonable use of natural resources and ecological concern for the planet. The adults entrust the young people with fixing in the future what they, the adults, are unwisely destroying today. Where will these sane new adults come from in the future, with today's children and teenagers heavily irradiated and influenced by the selfishness of pragmatic business?

Consumer culture encourages the consumption of products and services and suggests that this is valuable to society. Overconsumption is valuable for business because it brings profit, but people do not really need to own too many material things. The negatives of overconsumption are well known, but they do not seem to worry those who should be making decisions about the future of our planet. Among the negative consequences of overproduction, it is enough to mention air pollution, the depletion of natural resources, the low quality of products to be able to buy again and low wages for workers. The culture of fast food, fast fashion, and fast education leads to a reduction in quality so that you can buy from the same market. We are all caught in the web, and it takes a lot of effort to get out.

Consumer culture is sweeping the world today and capturing the minds of children and teenagers. A lot of purposeful work is needed in this direction, jointly at home and at school, to divert children's attention from consumption, as they believe this is the only way to feel happy. This is possible only if children and adolescents are surrounded by intelligent, reasonable, and spiritually developed adults, for whom the valuable things in life are not measured only by the amount of salary you receive.

Children need to know about the duality of human nature. They deserve to know from a young age that our biological body and our spiritual body need different types of stimuli and food for existence and development.   It is true, unfortunately, that schools today reflect society's consumer culture. The competition, the pursuit of high scores, the private lessons, all are in a race to achieve results calculated in percentages. The pressure to attend a prestigious university and then to find a well-paid job continues on. Schools today around the world are largely subordinated to a consumer culture that captures their minds from school with promises of social success expressed in greater salaries. How does one resist all this temptation? As a result, however, children go through schools as factories for diplomas and certificates but are completely deprived of the opportunity to develop the spiritual side of their nature. Many young people do not even know it exists at all. The greed of adults is to blame in this.

Material and spiritual development must go hand in hand and children have a right to know about it. For this, they need educated adults who themselves continue to develop spiritually. Adults who care about discovering children's talents and individually work with them to develop them. Children's talents should be shown to the world in order to give children self-confidence, that even intangible things are worth working for. To know that intangible rewards give us sensations, emotions and experiences that cannot be compared to any material reward. Admiration, respect, pride - this must be cultivated and developed.

Consumption cannot make us happy, on the contrary, it creates unhappy people who are only focused on materialism. Consumption does not develop us harmoniously and comprehensively, because it is concentrated only on buying and selling. It does not touch our heart or soul, rather, it glides over the surface of dead matter. It creates a one-dimensional reality of people who are perceived only as biological robots, hidden behind the mask of successful and happy consumers. Human nature is reflected in a distorted form, inferior and limited, as is the nature of the piles of objects that business forces us to constantly buy. This creates frivolous, superficial people unable to exercise independence or critical thinking because they blindly trust that businesses know what they need to be happy. The consumer culture is not interested in our development as spiritual persons, because this is something that cannot be expressed in percentages and exact results, and it takes time to achieve, and as a result it does not bring profit. Therefore, consumer culture completely and deliberately ignores the spiritual side of human nature. We are only important to the extent that we have the cash to buy their product and service.

The mirrors of the consumer society are limited in their ability to reflect the whole person with all their needs, not only the material ones. Is there a bigger scam for people than so-called 'shopping therapy' and similar traps to spend more money?

Behind the masks of social well-being, expensive cars, luxurious tourist destinations, lies the fear and insecurity of our present-day existence, refusing to see and be active for its overall development. Adults have this sin today in front of children, who are caught in the trap of consumption from childhood.

Consumption will never solve the conflict that is inherent in the dualism of human nature. Children and adolescents are particularly affected. It is no coincidence that the number of people with mental problems is growing, as is the business of services offered by psychotherapists. Consumer mental health is something that cannot be balanced with buying and selling. It is known how around certain holidays such as Christmas and others, the aggression of business advertisements begins a few months in advance to warm up consumers to buy more goods. Goods are also thematically packaged for the respective holiday. Around Christmas, it is suggested every year that you must achieve a supreme state of happiness, well-being and some unearthly ecstasy, the beginning of which is hysterically counted down in days and hours. When that otherworldly happiness does not come, you are left cowering, scared, lonely, broken, and unable to pick up the pieces to move forward with your life. At this point, the idea of shopping therapy sounds cynical against the backdrop of the number of single people, who feel guilty that they cannot meet business expectations and meet their fictional standards of happiness. Many people get really depressed and have a hard time with these holidays because they feel guilty that they cannot live up to these made-up hysterical expectations. It is time for people to wake up and see the true face of advertising and the business intent behind it. All this crazy counting down of days and hours until Friday night, until the start of the magical vacation, are ways of fragmenting our lives and ways of telling us that we live only by consuming.

How can education change the picture of today's consumer society? By clarifying the specifics of the consumer society, what it gives us, but also what it takes away from us, its advantages, and disadvantages. With a constant emphasis on the duality of human nature, both material and spiritual. Adolescents must develop a critical and reasonable attitude towards this consumer mass culture.

The psychological side effects of consumerism are many, and the most affected are adolescents and young people, who have not yet built in themselves stability and endurance, which are part of spiritual riches. The realisation that they do not yet have the monetary resources to own all this useless matter that is aggressively advertised, leads to low self-esteem and doubts about their worthiness as a person. It can lead to anxiety, envy, and depression. Social media is a part of the lives of teenagers today, and through it, advertisements are like the insidious agents of business that are everywhere. Their messages can be destructive because they instil the idea that your personal happiness depends on how many things you can buy. This leads to frustration, because at the age of teenagers their personal wealth is not expressed in money. Focusing only on material things leads to selfishness, competition, envy, greed, lack of empathy, complacency, superficiality, and cruelty.

Business messages and advertisements do not emphasise the spiritual side of human nature as a decisive factor in achieving personal happiness. The business has no interest in such messages reaching us, the consumers, because in order to achieve personal happiness, harmony, gratitude, mental balance you do not need to give any money to anyone. These are states of the human soul that everyone can develop for themselves, and the price is personal discipline. This is why businesses are emphasising consumerism, as they want us to believe that this will make us consumers happy, but in essence it just makes them richer. This is a particularly dangerous philosophy for the age of adolescents, who themselves cannot yet judge what is true and what is not but are willing to experiment. If they do not have adults around them who know how to develop their energies on a spiritual level, then unfortunately they will be blind to this side of human nature. School, as an institution, is the place that is obliged to cultivate and develop the spirituality of young people. Teachers should pay attention not only to the results of the subject they teach, but also to developing parallel humanistic qualities within adolescents. Adolescents should know that happiness is the ability of a person to feel and see the world around them in a pleasant way. We all have the innate ability to do so, to identify sources of happiness and joy. There is joy in giving, sharing your inner riches with others, rejoicing in the talents of others, supporting them on their path to success, lending a helping hand to a friend in need, showing compassion and nobility to every person. This is all possible, regardless of how wealthy or 'socially' levelled an individual is.

To instil this, adults must encourage these behaviours, daily. These treasures of the human soul are completely free and capable of making us permanently joyful, regardless of whether we have the money to buy the latest model of phones. These topics are sensitive for teenagers and this needs to be explained. We all want tomorrow's generation to have qualities which home in on spirituality, altruism and humans full of empathy. The identification of teenagers should not be associated with objects and possessions of which they can afford to buy, but with all the cosmic intelligence around us, it should be based on the energy they draw from. This will lead to a deeper and greater understanding of the essence of life processes, and also of our leading role in these processes. Not only as passive selfish consumers, but as active producers of joy, gratitude, charity, benevolence, and mutual aid.

EMOTIONS AS A DEFENCE MECHANISM FOR SURVIVAL

Human emotions are those mediators between us and other living beings, which serve to convey our attitude expressed through our facial expressions and body language. Our smile and our eyes often speak more than any words could ever do. The gestures we use and our body language in general, all express how we feel in any given moment. In many situations, it is important for us that others know how we feel, and vice versa, as through the emotions of others, we can understand what is happening to them at the moment. Are we happy, sad, cheerful, in love, angry or scared? Our emotions can help us convey these feelings.

Some of the emotions are common to us humans and to other living beings. They are the universal language that all living beings speak, and which needs no translation. For example, in animals such as dogs, we observe their emotions in their actions. Often when they are angry or scared, they may bare their teeth or bite. On the contrary, when they are happy, they may wag their tail and jump around. In observing these emotions from a dog, we are equipped with how to respond. For instance, when a dog is happy to meet us, it is usually because he/she recognises and approves of us, and associates us as a friend. There is no threat. However, if the dog is angry, it is a sure signal to us that this may be a threat to us. Adequate recognition of certain emotions, such as fear, joy, and anger, is linked to our physical survival. At this level, humans are similar to other living beings. Our ability to adequately read the emotions that other people express is extremely important to relationships and to our survival. This is what children should learn.

Correct reading of emotions and adequate reactions to them is part of our emotional intelligence. Part of it is whether we can express empathy in the moment where we need to. Many animal species, such as gorillas and chimpanzees, are also capable of expressing empathy through their emotions and body language. Primates are also capable of expressing, whether it is through a pat on the back, a hug, an attempt at a smile, or even a twinkle in the eye. Curiosity, empathy, altruism, reconciliation, affection, and emotions connect us to other biological species, and are born of maternal care. The maternal instinct to preserve the species, along with search for food, reproduction, and the desire to dominate, are common to humans and animals.

However, a person is capable of more than adequately expressing their emotions. A person is able to consciously hide their emotions, i.e., by not expressing through their body language or facial expressions. This means that a person can control the manifestation of their emotions. Why do we need to control our emotions? The reasons are many and it depends on what emotions we are trying to hide and what is the reason that gave rise to them. If it is joy, we may not want others to know about it. If it is anger, showing it can provoke anger on the other side and lead to physical harm.

Controlling our emotions is extremely important for teenagers. They must learn this, because at this age they often vacillate from one extreme to the other. They are either exalted to the point of hysterics, or they are angry, sad, and depressed. Very often anger gets outside of them and serves as a spark that can ignite a major conflict between them and others. How do we learn to balance their emotions and frequent mood swings?

There are so many challenges in adolescent life that provoke strong emotional reactions. These could be hormonal changes, a brain that is still developing, intensity of social interactions with their peers, academic demands, and high expectations of their parents. Many teens also struggle with body image issues, strained relationships with family members, and an over-reliance on technology in favour of face-to-face contact. Online addiction can greatly affect how they interact in real life with others, to the point of avoiding such interactions altogether, and towards social isolation and fear. In addition, depression, anxiety, and eating disorders can cause real mental health problems. Desperation, anger, fear or confusion can also cause a block in adolescents for a long time.

Learning to accept what they are experiencing in the moment is important. They must understand that they have the right to experience negative emotions and there is nothing wrong with that. However, adolescents must learn to control their emotions, so that they do not become obsessed with one type of emotion. Life itself is like a huge wave that sometimes overwhelms us, and we feel like we are disappearing. Other times we are on top and manage to balance like surfers. Denying and refusing to accept what we are experiencing can be more dangerous to our psyche. Resistance brings suffering that sometimes consumes us with its strength and intensity, and if it stays with us for a long time, it can turn into depression. Adults must accept the idea that teenagers can suffer from depression, a right that some often deny their children. This is also part of underestimating children's personality and not knowing them at all.

Meditation is a phenomenon that enables us to consciously stay in the moment, one where we can take a break out of the recurrent cycle of one's thoughts and emotions. This is what teenagers need. Teenagers need an adult to introduce them to the magical world of meditation. Deep breathing techniques are only one part of meditation, and they have a positive effect and can improve both concentration and calmness.

Adults must admit that we ourselves very often quickly lose self-control, get angry and fail to maintain composure in critical situations. Often this happens in communication with our adolescents, however we should show adolescents how to manage and regulate their emotions as an example to them. It is imperative that adults display positive regulating behaviours when it comes to their emotions, as adolescents will mimic this and regulate within the same manner. It is important to emphasise that controlling ourselves does not mean suggesting to adolescents that this is how we hide our emotions or even hypocritically denying that nothing can throw us off balance. This is not the point of self-control. During these emotional storms, we often say things that can hurt others. Sometimes we are like a loaded gun that fires words in directions that hurt other people and us. This is what happens if we fail to control ourselves. There must be ethical boundaries that we must not cross, and everyone must be aware of this in advance. In this regard, it is good to familiarise adolescents with what the physical symptoms of strong anger are, for example, and what they should do first to stop it.

The human body reacts to the storm inside us, our heart rate increases, our hands sweat, our face turns red, and we feel as if we are trembling and plugged into the electrical system. Perhaps the most sensible thing in this case is to step back and get away from the situation that provokes anger. Counting and taking deep breaths are the initial brakes that can help keep the volcano from erupting. If anger is the emotion that teenagers experience most often and that can scare them with its intensity, then it might be a good idea for adults to make an appointment with a professional psychologist to suggest other coping strategies. In such situations, it is not appropriate to punish the adolescent for the way they feel, as this will send the wrong signals to them. In the long term, sports, music, and creativity are able to transform negative energy into positive energy and balance the psyche. Avoiding the negative temptations that provoke anger is also a way to avoid it.

Mental health is part of a person's overall health and teenagers should know this. Especially emotions and our inability to control them within acceptable, healthy limits, can lead to deterioration of our health. This will reflect on our physical body with headaches, palpitations, inability to breathe and even more serious problems with some organs of the body. That is why it is so important to develop mental toughness in adolescents. Being resistant to negative emotions means that they pass through them more easily and quickly, and they do not experience them deeply and do not carry them in their thoughts for a long time.

Part of mental resilience is the way we look at the problems that happen to us. Whether we dwell on them for a long time or accept the fact that only things we like can happen to us, we learn to find a practical solution to the problem. Shifting the focus will help us shift the focus from the dramatic experience to the action. Combined with the understanding that only one who does nothing makes no mistakes will help us to get up quickly after each fall and move on. Knowing our strengths and weaknesses will help us to be realistic in different situations and neither underestimate nor overestimate our abilities, so as not to lead to dramatic disappointments. Accepting other people as they are, not as we wish them to be, will help us not to mince words and start explaining relationships every time someone does something we do not like.

There are many ways to build mental resilience, but all of them require a certain spiritual discipline and the realisation that you want to become stronger so that you do not give up but keep fighting. Teenagers need adults to share all these things with them to help them develop them within themselves. Therefore, together with the practice of self-control, one must also develop resilience, endurance of the psyche, so that nervous crises do not become a part of everyday life.

It is especially difficult for adolescents who have certain mental illnesses, such as autism spectrum disorder (ASD). They are particularly affected by different types of conflict situations, and human relationships in general can prove to be a real test for them. Especially with regards to the adequate reading of emotions. Specialist psychologists should work with them to help them learn how to deal with typical situations, how to understand the emotional signals of others and how to transmit their own emotional waves in a way that can be understood correctly. This is a real challenge for them, which can doom them to social isolation and loneliness. In this sense, we come to the conclusion that emotions are extremely important for our social survival and they are part of our survival mechanisms. They are our subtle tools that we must learn how to use in order not to hurt people, but to make them fall in love with our personality.

Classical music should be used as background music at home and at school, so it will naturally enter the lives of adolescents. If you ask them if they would consciously listen to classical music, they will most likely laugh because, according to their stereotypes, it is the type of music that old people listen to. So, make it a part of their life, non-violently and naturally, and it may make them calm and bring them closer to the layers of culture. This will make them part of the history and nature of classical music in a beautiful and festive way. Once they hear classical music, teenagers will be hungry for more and that can harmonise and balance their inner world and mental health. This will make them joyful, calm, and confident as people who do not give up after the first lost battle but continue to build their life with all its ups and downs. Merging with nature is another powerful meditative tool of returning to ourselves.

STRIVING FOR DEVELOPMENT

Growth goes hand in hand with development and is the accumulation of life experience and knowledge. Development is inherent in every form of life. Development is related to the expansion of the body and our inner world, and this leads to learning, and knowing. For this purpose, nothing needs to be done, nature drives these processes. Natural elements govern human life, behaviour and thinking. These energies come from space, through nature and include humans. There are several aspirations, energy trends, spontaneous reactions and movements that are common to the entire cosmos and to humans. These are striving for development and expansion, striving for freedom, striving for inclusiveness, and striving for dominance.

In education and upbringing, most conflicts arise from a misunderstanding of how significant these elements are to us, small and large. Just as the macrocosm is constantly expanding and breaking down its old forms, limitations, and frameworks, and expanding its identity, so too do humans. We are never satisfied with what we have, as humans we always want more. The moment we achieve our dream, it is no longer interesting to us. We are driven by the drive for development and expansion, much like the ever-expanding cosmos around us. The limitations and social frameworks that others place on us make us rebel and reject them, because we are driven by our desire for freedom, just as the cosmos around us strives for limitlessness.

Adults must know how to harness these forces to be useful and effective for learners, non-violently, but respectfully as free persons. Human life is like a mirror of the cosmic and the natural. Much of the conflict in intergenerational relationships results from a misunderstanding of these driving elements, and from the desire of adults to forcibly limit freedom and development by imposing overcontrol and restrictions. How can the socially acceptable be reconciled with the idea of liberation from constraints and the expansion of identity, so that we can justly and democratically use their power for development? We adults need to learn how to negotiate with teenagers, cooperate and persuade them, not fight against them, and resist their ideas just because we do not like them.

These general energies and trends of development are manifested, from the great, vast, constantly changing and expanding cosmos, through the development of the planet. Through the development of plants and animals, the development of people, and the specificities and sameness in the development of human beings. They make us an integral part of the laws of the development of the universe, of the big picture, encompassing everything in one whole energy structure. The cosmos, universe, planets, stars, animals, plants, inanimate (supposedly) matter, nature, and people. Even inanimate matter changes, which means that there is some form of life or energy in it.

Development includes the knowledge that adults often stop, guided only by what they consider important. Either way, we cannot stop the expansion that involves development, growth, and learning. Everything changes, transforms, energy is not lost but it takes new forms. Everything is in a continuous process of change, movement and development in a direction predetermined by cosmic intelligence. The direction of development of living beings and of man is marked by cyclicity.

In this sense, our children are cosmic messengers whose development we cannot and must not stop. The point is not to be a hindrance or a brake on this majestic path of cosmic expansion. The role of adults in this cosmic project is to guide children wisely and consciously towards improvement and adaptation to social norms and rules. By preserving their inner personal freedom, which is the main condition for spiritual development, it is also characteristic of the cosmos that every form is the penultimate form. The same applies to humans, that everything we want is the penultimate thing. We are in a constant process of searching, expanding, and our little personal 'big bangs' are the explosions, without which, there is no development to a new level. These energy aspirations are the foundation of our spiritual growth.

The development of the innate abilities of adolescents occurs in the process of overcoming difficulties and contradictions. Adolescents intuitively seek and find those pivotal moments that change them. Nature directs them to conflict situations and difficulties in order to change and overcome them. This powerful developmental impulse takes hold of children as an element over which they do not control, and which often makes them part of antics and dangerous ventures. The pedagogical task of adults is that, while learning, the adolescent is constantly faced with the need to overcome various types of difficulties. These difficulties are tailored to their individual capabilities.

In this sense, each child strives to develop, following the impulses and their inner voice, which is their connection with the great cosmos. Development is like a vast sphere filled with an infinite number of grains of possibility, just as the universe that creates the situations and circumstances for each of us is infinite. If the environment is favourable, the grains germinate. If not, then they wither and die. What environment does a grain of knowledge need? It needs the presence of knowledgeable people around it, and the examples and images that these people will give. Like breeds like. For example, what kind of environment is needed for that seed of love to grow? A loving environment is needed, adults are needed to show examples of how to love. Children are our mirrors, and adolescents are at a stage when they not only reflect, but also test these mirrors, critically observe, and look for their own ways to develop the grains of knowledge.

Development is a process of revealing all the kernels embedded within the child. An important aspect of growing these beans is difficult. They are necessary for children to overcome and develop. We know that children are creatures that constantly seek difficulties and challenges. Overcoming difficulties, the child experiences joy and happiness. Adventures are that path that they themselves start and that they do not stop until they satisfy their curiosity and their thirst for knowledge. This does not apply to such difficulties as control by adults, which is often a brake on the path of knowledge. Adults are less likely to seek difficulties, because they have already passed this path and are following their new cycle. In the desire to control the teenager's every move is often hidden the desire of adults to protect the teenager from possible mistakes and disappointments. Adults know from experience that this can happen. Humans are so structured that they learn only from their own mistakes, but not from the mistakes of others. Therefore, over-control leads to a halt in the development process. Adolescents prefer to learn from their experiences, seeking their own ways and challenges, regardless of the patronage of adults. So, they intuitively look for activities where they can get it. These are often dangerous activities. The task of adults is to create a safe environment in which the adolescent will overcome difficulties that contribute to the acquisition of useful experience and development. This is regardless of the mistakes that adolescents will make, because it will be their mistakes that will also give them valuable experience.

Inseparably connected with the desire for development is the desire for growth, which is also laid down by nature in every living form of life. A child is not born to remain a child forever. Children are usually more mature than we like to see them. This is confirmed by role-playing games, in which the child takes on the 'duties' of an adult. Childhood is not a frozen state of carelessness, a golden time when you do not have to worry about anything. Real childhood is a complex and is sometimes a painful process of growing up. The satisfaction of this passion occurs in communication, mostly with adults. By compartmentalising children in boxes, stating that they are 'still small' and its corresponding attitudes contradict the natural laws of development that drive children and push them forward to experiment. However, the actions based on the statement of 'you are old enough', serve to create conditions for active manifestation and satisfaction of the passion for growth. Adults should communicate with the child on an equal footing, affirm their personality, entrust them with important things and cooperate with them. However, children go to school not to continue their games there, but to establish themselves there in their growth. Children should be educated not playfully, but seriously, with a sense of responsibility. This is even more true of the complex and contradictory nature of adolescence, often full of conflicts and insurmountable misunderstandings.

Adolescents want to be like adults in order to be valued and accepted as equals by them. That is why it is so important for them to be allowed to experiment, to embark on adventures, from which they will gain valuable experience. It is therefore necessary for their growth and accumulation of knowledge. Without the inner desire to be an adult, the process of growing up would not take place and children are truly inspired to be taken seriously as adults.

Adolescents are often offended when adults treat them like small children, which means they underestimate and belittle them. This can have the opposite effect of making them lose the desire to try if they are stopped every time by adults. Thus, they can become passive, timid, inert and submissive. Children will then mimic a puppet that adult's control. Imagine every time the teenager wants to share something different, something provocative and critical. Imagine how every time the adolescent wants to use their hands and feet for activities that the adult will not approve of, they, the adult, ties up both their hands and feet. Is this what we want from our children? To become obedient puppets that we control, and then blame them for not being proactive, brave, and enterprising. How do they develop initiative when every time they want to do something, we as adults run to stop their inner urge? Gradually, the adults turn into rigid, conservative grumblers who, at any cost, want to turn the teenagers into the same. We are so afraid of losing control that we forget that it kills the vital energies of development and turns teenagers into obedient puppets.

They will respect us more if we make them feel like adults, more mature than they really are. They will want to communicate with us more and more if we are interested in what they say and if we take it seriously. Adolescents strive for the feeling of adulthood, but without the responsibility that comes with it. All children want to grow up as soon as possible. It is the adult's job to teach them that growing up and responsibilities go hand in hand. The important thing is that adults do not kill these aspirations, but skilfully nurture and stimulate them.

The drive for expansion is related to the development of life, which cannot be stopped. Even if we try to stop adolescents from trying and experimenting in order to gain life experience, they will continue to do so, but without us. This is because they will see us as a brake on their development path. Nothing can stop development and life. Everything around us is in a constant process of expansion, whether it be physical, emotional, creative, or intellectual. In this sense, we see the expansion in adolescents as the accumulation and expansion of social and life experience and knowledge, as independent personal and creative growth.

The processes of growth, development and expansion are the basis of life processes and cycles. Adults cannot stop them, even if they try. Any attempt to redirect the vital energy in a direction not chosen by the adolescent, may meet with resistance that comes from the inner impulses of development. This moves us away from the great cosmos. What adults, both at school and in the family, can do is to try to make friends with teenagers so that they are allowed to be part of the exciting adventure of growing up that nature itself pushes them towards. Any attempt to stop these processes and curiosity can lead to conflicts, alienation, and arrest in development. Spiritual growth also depends on how brave we are, continuously looking for what is hidden behind the obvious material, visible to the eyes. Only in this constant forward movement is the meaning of life. The joy of life is in the movement, the discovery, the conquest, and the continuation to the next peak. Any stagnation is a slow death.

STRIVING FOR FREEDOM AND INDEPENDENCE

Freedom is defined as the right to act, speak, or think as you wish without being punished. The pursuit of freedom and independence is at the core of human nature. This drive is driven by impulses stronger than ourselves. Freedom and happiness are two sensations that do not exist outside of us, and they do not exist in the external physical world. They are part of our understanding of what our place and right to voice among other people is and how we feel about it. Freedom is one of the main reasons people fight to regain it. The feeling of the lack of freedom appears when something of ours is taken away or we are forbidden to do and say openly what we want. In such situations, universally people resist change. Often this is accompanied by bloodshed and violence. Occupying territory, being jailed for saying what the government does not want to hear, over-controlling our actions and deeds, are good reasons to rebel to regain the right to do as we want, but respecting moral and ethical norms.

The quest for freedom is inextricably linked with the quest for growth, development and expansion. The moment we acquire something and call it 'ours' or 'mine', is the moment that humans want to be freed from it, so that it does not suppress our individual freedom. We are constantly expanding on every level, and nothing is enough for us. At the heart of this element is the desire for creative development. It is desirable that adults are spiritually and creatively developed in order to support this aspiration and curiosity in children. Nothing we have is enough for us, we always want more and especially what we do not have.

It depends on what kind of people the adults want to raise, are they free and creative, or are they obedient and mechanically fulfilling other people's orders. Free people have always been a thorn in the side of society, and this also applies to adults - in school and family. They seek to raise dependent people, obedient people to fit into certain moulds and labels. Why not strive to educate free people who will create new realities and help our consciousness to expand? Why are adults so afraid of it?

Basic to this age are these two elements of expansion and freedom. Why do adults, when it comes to themselves, insist that these two aspirations for development and freedom be respected by others.

They themselves seek to silence them in children and adolescents. Are they afraid of the freedom-loving teenagers and their desire for independence? Are they trying to stop time?

What methods can help adults not to kill these two aspirations in adolescents, but to nurture and cultivate them, which will eliminate conflicts between generations? This is also related to the upbringing of adults themselves, because only free adults who strive to constantly develop can nurture such aspiration in other people. How can these two elements be used so that the process of education and training is conflict-free and successful, creative, and not commanding? In school, the pursuit of development is suffocated by a lack of creativity in the learning process, there is only mechanical memorisation. The pursuit of freedom is generally considered dangerous for adults, both in the family and at school and they strive to raise obedient children.

How do we as adults transform naughty and rebellious energy into creative energy? Therefore, adults are needed who consciously know how to develop their own creative energy. Creative teachers are needed, not just command-and-authoritarian ones who care more about the rules than the learners. The individual parts and stages of the lesson structure should be constantly revised and a place for a creative approach should be found in them. Why do adults often seek to kill these two drives instead of using them in the educational process? Allow teenagers to participate in legislating the rules and they will not rebel against them.

The two natural elements, forces and energies govern our lives, regardless of our age. The more adults try to suppress them in children, the more they breed rebellion and resistance in them. The two elements go hand in hand and complement each other. The specificity of these two elements should be known by adults and used in the process of education and training. The powerful energy of these two elements must be transformed into a constructive and creative one, in building personal qualities. Yet why is this not happening? If you stop these two natural elements, forces, and powerful energies that arise in us without knowing how, you also stop life. This is the specificity of life, in its constant free expansion and development. In the constant breaking and expanding of the limitations, is the set and petrified comfortable identity that stops our development. This is because it is part of a compulsive cycle that adults skilfully take care not to break. These two elements are part of a greater inclusivity in which we consciously, with heart, soul, attention, and care participate and involve ourselves in every manifestation of life.

The quest for freedom must be seen in the context of evolutionary processes. Or maybe our understanding of freedom as a social and personal category is outdated and it is time to look at this powerful impulse towards independence on a larger scale? Shouldn't freedom be seen as a reflection of the evolution of our own consciousness? Our notion of freedom and independence is as great and important as our own evolution of our consciousness. In this sense, freedom is also an evolutionary category. As an evolutionary category, freedom is not a right that is given to us by someone, because historically in human society, everything illustrates the desire for freedom to be taken away, it is not given. Perhaps, if we raise it to the rank of an evolutionary category, only then will we recognise freedom as our duty, which we ourselves must win and keep for ourselves. Our need for freedom and independence will be reciprocal to our own spiritual growth and needs.

There are many examples of people who do not feel the need to be free and independent from other people and circumstances, because they themselves have not yet matured to the idea of what they need this for and what exactly they can do with their own independence. There are also many cases when these processes are deliberately stopped because our own immaturity and lack of confidence and lack of spiritual growth make us afraid to continue developing without the patronage and direction given to us by other people. This means that evolutionarily this type of person has not matured to the need to want to be free and independent from other people. On the contrary, it is possible that they strive with all their might to remain in the shadow provided by their patrons, to remain in the cage. Therefore, we think that if we proclaim freedom as an evolutionary category, then everyone will feel obliged to fight for it. All according to their own needs. You cannot make someone independent if they do not understand the need for it. Adolescents are at a stage of development when nature pushes them to break free from the chains of adults. They boldly and courageously become intoxicated with the idea of their own independence from the world of adults.

What does freedom mean to teenagers? It means the freedom to do whatever they want, just like adults. It means the freedom to not have their every move controlled and directed. The freedom to choose their friends, regardless of whether their parents will disapprove of their choice and the negative influence that comes with it. The freedom to experiment, even with their own sexuality. The freedom in school enables one to choose whom they sit next to, to voice their disapproval of the teachers' methods and to be critical of the institution of the school.

Freedom for them is related to breaking social rules, norms, restrictions, frameworks, stereotypes, and prejudices set by adults. We subconsciously and consciously always try to remove the restrictions and break the frames in which society puts us, we try to be free and independent.

There is a reversal of roles, as teenagers want what adults have. They want to dominate, to set the tone, to assign roles and to say how things should happen. They want to be adults. Adults should allow them to practice this, but also teach them how to be aware of their responsibilities as well.

Freedom is important for teenagers because it emphasises their individuality and independence. This is a step in the direction of life outside the family and school nest, where adults decide what is good for them. They know that they are still financially dependent on their parents, but even this chain cannot stop them from rebelling against the system. Growing up is the perfect time to get carried away by an idea and a cause and fight for it. It is the time to resist every injustice and lie, driven by the pure idealism of your age.

This enormous energy must be used by adults, so that it is not wasted and lost, but as fuel to fuel the transformation of adolescents into freedom-loving adults. There is certainly no adult who does not secretly envy the independent spirit and idealism that teenagers bring. They have not yet fully adopted the form of social restrictions and prohibitions, to know what it is like to fear losing a job and a salary, as an example. The desire to be independent is an urge that comes from our inner voice, and it is our direct connection to the voice of nature. The drive for freedom connects us with the rest of the biological species that suffer and lose their vital energy when they are confined for a long time in a cage.

Is it dangerous to give teenagers too much freedom? This answer may be individual for everyone. Adults should not stop urges for independence but should inform the younger generation of what negative consequences certain actions may have. Therefore, we think it is important for adults to explain to adolescents why freedom is an evolutionary category as well and how its understanding depends on the level of our own civilizational evolution of our consciousness. With the right to do, speak and think as we please, comes the obligation not to transgress ethical and moral boundaries that harm other people.

A sense of freedom can be fostered in adolescents through the right to choose similar things, rather than having ready-made solutions imposed on them. This feeling can be nurtured in many ways and is based on the dialogue, negotiation, and

213

compromises that the adult and adolescent will make. Especially in school, which by its very nature is a coercive process. There are only a few teenagers who frankly share that if their parents do not force them to go to school, they will not enter this institution. There are many reasons why some teenagers do not want to go to school and why they do not feel happy there. Part of these reasons lies in the very nature of school; it is a place where teenagers have no choice and freedom. They just have to do what they are told. They do not choose their subjects, their teachers, or their exams. The teacher must be a true virtuoso in their profession to understand this contradiction and try to give freedom of choice to the adolescents. Therefore, distinguishing the school as an institution is perceived by adolescents as freedom. Unfortunately, many leave school before taking their final exams, which leads to problems related to their professional realization in the future. This is a problem that is born as a result of the spontaneous decision to run away from the place where you do not feel joyful. One of the reasons is related to low academic results, which directly affect the self-esteem of adolescents. This can provoke a desire to distance yourself from the place where you are not appreciated as you would like. As a result, there is a feeling of injustice and a desire to escape from that place.

Equal communication with adolescents and mutual respect can mitigate the sense of being in a cage, that school can leave with some learners. Adults must explain that there is freedom of spirit, inner freedom, and independence. It can also be achieved even in conditions of restrictions and lack of external freedom. It is part of the spiritual growth of the individual. It has to do with mastering the ability to mentally distance themselves from others and perceive themselves as an individual. Meditation techniques help one to establish and discover their own individuality by understanding their separateness from everything around them. Thus, the desire to distance ourselves from what oppresses and limits us is naturally connected to the desire for freedom and independence, as a way to establish ourselves in what we want and think.

The desire for distancing can also be a trap for adolescents who, in their desire to feel unique and different from others. It may even reach extreme cases of distinguishing themselves from their peers. They shut down, cut off communication, get depressed and lose touch with the world. Lack of social experience pushes them to extremes that may be dangerous in their attractiveness. This is why different techniques for different types of meditations are one of the most successful and healthy ways to both separate and distance yourself with your spirit from others, so as not to unify yourself. On the contrary, it serves to preserve the freedom of your spirit, and to remain part of the society without which we cannot exist anyway. A complete separation from society is impossible without suffering our psyche and adequate perception of reality. We are part of everything living and non-living around us, and we are not something isolated and self-sufficient. Therefore, we must find a way to feel joyful and free within the life we are given. This is a huge privilege that can only be realised through freedom of spirit.

MEDITATION AS A PATH TO SPIRITUAL GROWTH

The history of meditation practices around the world is thousands of years old, and it is the result of a person's desire to look beyond the material. It is to understand what is hidden behind the visible and obvious, to find the way to oneself. Curiosity about all that is beyond our biological needs has led to remarkable observations that different cultures have shaped into different spiritual theories and developmental practices. This is a sure path that leads to spiritual development. The benefits of meditation are many and they are already known to those who are interested in them. The various meditation practices are an ideal means of achieving mental equilibrium and balance, inner harmony, and relaxation. They are tools that can help one to develop good personal discipline if you do not already have it.

Humans, driven by their inner drives and impulses, which are our connection to the energy of cosmic intelligence, have left shining examples of various meditation practices over the centuries. Some of them, such as prayer, are part of the religions of the world. Others have taken their own path in people's lives as systems of exercise and breathing techniques, shaping a philosophy of how to perceive life in its entirety. As a result of all of them, the collective consciousness of people is developed, which, as an accumulation, leads to insights about our relationship with the larger cosmos. Additionally, it leads to an insight in how to draw energy from it in order to live our earthly life beautifully and spiritually. This is the other great benefit of meditation practices, as they make us a part of everything which is around us. Meditation also unites us, and it becomes part of our emotionality and experiences. So, we can absorb the energy of a plant, for example, energetically become a plant and feel the beauty and aroma of its colours as a part of ourselves. This is because we are also those colours and aromas. We can become a majestic tree and feel its durability and resilience as a part of ourselves. Whenever we are having a hard time, we can be inspired by the magnificent trees around us. We can be anything, the rushing water that wants to reach the other bridge to tell what it has seen and heard, the butterfly that has just survived the death of the chrysalis to be born out of pain and suffering. We can be the wind that carries all the news around the world. We can be the hot sun whose rays warm us when our heart is cold after a breakup. We may also mimic the hot snow that comes after nothing else is left.

This meditative practice of transforming and taking on another image can help us develop empathy, mercy, and compassion for all around us. It can help us develop a sense of responsibility, so that we will better protect the things around us if they are a part of ourselves. Thus, our life will never end because there are so many great creations around whose lives we share. In this sense, we become immortal. As a result, we will feel our life becoming more saturated and interesting, because everything around us becomes a part of ourselves. This inevitably leads to an expansion of our own identity, giving us volume and exciting significance. We will learn how to experience, not just analyse.

Meditation practices help to stay here and now, to feel it and to experience it. They help us stop and be alone with ourselves to hear everything we need in the silence of our body and psyche. It is achieved by focusing the mind for a period of time on one thing, in silence or with the help of chanting, for religious and spiritual purposes or as a method of relaxation. It is about training in awareness and gaining a healthy sense of perspective. Consciously choosing to experience this moment now, enables us to fully surrender to it. Try not to shut out your thoughts or feelings and learn to observe without judgment. Eventually, you might start to understand them better.

In a deep sense, meditation is a tool of the spiritual teachings of Buddhism that helps clear the mind and learn how to control it. This allows one to achieve an inner state of peace of mind and body with full awareness and attention. There are different meditation practices. Some focus on relaxation and non-judgmental observation of the present moment of existence. Others have a specific object in the form of thoughts and sensations and are often combined with visualisation. The purpose of such meditations is to control not only consciousness, but also our inner energy.

Looking at meditation from a more down-to-earth perspective, for those who lead an active lifestyle, the practices can become a resource for physical and emotional recovery. This happens as a result of the deep relaxation of the muscles and the achievement of peace of mind and feelings. In addition, meditation can improve attention and concentration during training and competition. Which, of course, will have a positive effect on academic results. Those who regularly practice meditation significantly expand their consciousness and the limits of perception of reality. Simply put, people live more brightly, feel happiness more strongly and much more often, because they can see the beauty in ordinary things. There is an opportunity to accept and release negative emotions and feelings while remaining in harmony. This teaches attention.

Choosing the right technique depends on personal preference. Meditate with your eyes open and closed. You can do it sitting, standing, lying down and even walking. The most important rule is to keep the spine straight, the chest free and keeping the physical body as relaxed as possible. Beginners can sit in a chair, lean back, and close their eyes. One just starts breathing, relaxing the muscles, and therefore relaxing their thoughts. It is necessary to maintain your usual frequency of breathing, you should not try to take longer breaths if you feel uncomfortable and strained by this. We inhale through the nose with the mouth closed, hold for a few seconds, and then exhale through the mouth, listening to the air stream that the nose and mouth produce. This repeats itself for several minutes, like waves and one after the other. Inhale and exhale slowly and deeply. After all, meditation implies love and reverence for oneself and the body, not violence. It is a rare moment when we can be alone with ourselves and with the very life within us. The more we practice, the more we will like these moments of silence within us, which are valuable in that they free us from all the burden of thoughts and emotions that the day has placed upon us.

The prompt to 'let go of your mind' sounds simple enough, but it is a very complex skill that takes practice. The main thing is to remember that for the first-time various fantasies, memories and anxious thoughts from everyday life will constantly come to mind. Therefore, distracting from the relaxation process. This is absolutely normal. Just gently switch your attention to breathing each time, do not get mad at yourself for not being able to concentrate, and do not think that you are doing something wrong. This is how it should be, as the brain cannot be empty, and it is closed for continuous reflection. Over time you will be able to be calm regardless of the thoughts that come and go, and you will learn how to concentrate solely on the air stream. Then the only thought you will have will be that you are breathing and that you exist. The only emotion, the joy of breathing, and the fact that you are alive. It is good to practice in the morning and evening, as well as at any time of the day when you feel tense. This fills the body with energy, calmness, resilience, and harmony, but also gives concentration.

Adolescents, with their restless spirits and energies that push them in different directions, with their conflicting extremes, emotional dramas and frequent mood swings and they need meditative practices. The benefits for them will be irreplaceable, they will help them calm down and will also fill them with patience and discipline. This tends to be lacking in the period of growing up. Practicing meditation regularly will teach them how to control their thoughts and emotions, and this will stop all the anxious buzzing in their heads. Many adolescents, driven by age-specific curiosity and experimentation, discover the world of meditation practices for themselves. This will change them forever because they will become part of the world of millennial techniques that will fill their personal little world with little magical discoveries about themselves and the world around them. The adventures of the spirit will make them open up and become sensitive to everything around them.

Unfortunately, in most schools there is no opportunity for teenagers to learn how to meditate. There is a lack of adults who can offer them this experience. As a result, schools become only a place that strains, stresses them and where someone always expects something from them. They are still not able to meet these expectations. The subject of meditation is absent. In private schools, there is a greater variety of extracurricular activities for children, which eases the burden of compulsory subjects. There are also a number of yoga centres that can be the first step into a world that introduces them to useful meditation techniques. Adolescents, with their curiosity and open senses to the world around them, need a philosophy that does not separate people on any basis, but unites them with everything around them. This philosophy offers an energy fusion whereby everything becomes a part of ourselves, and we expand our volume to infinity.

Meditation practices will help them relax, recover from a hard day at school and find joy in the little things. It is often thought that meditation is only suitable for professional yogis and people who want to know the hidden meanings of the universe. In fact, such practices are imperceptibly present in the daily life of each of us, because each of us is curious about what is invisible to the eyes. After all, we always strive to relax and get rid of stressful thoughts after work, training, or a fun vacation. Taking deep breaths is something that is done all over the world and is associated with relaxation. In order to achieve the maximum effect, one must know the individual breathing techniques.

We believe that in the schools of the future, the competitiveness and consumerism that still prevails will co-exist with feelings of solidarity, freedom, joy, and gratitude. In principle, there is nothing wrong with competition, because it naturally exists in nature. The competitive principle of who has more food, territory and spheres of influence is not from yesterday. These are the main forces that drive animals in general, our closest primate relatives and us humans. Look into your own life and realise where all your efforts are going throughout the day. In fact, they go to do things, such as working to earn money to cover their basic biological needs, including food, housing, and clothing. A small portion of it goes to entertainment and intellectual stimulation, which can lead to our own upgrading. Competition means there are fewer resources and opportunities, and more people want them. This leads to the desire to cover the benchmarks to be the chosen one. This is formally related to covering certain academic indicators and results. They place competition on a fair footing. Whoever has the highest academic achievement wins. Of course, there are exceptions where the order is sometimes messed up and the influence of connections, patronage, and corruption, for instance. This affects the outcome of the competition, but we are asked to consider this rather as an exception. So day after day, us adults become caught in this trap that we spin every day, continuously like robots. There are no happy, joyful, or free people in this trap. There are stressed, anxious and unhappy faces, on which pain and suffering become part of the social mask, covered with a thin transparent filter of frozen smile. This is supposed to demonstrate our civility and good manners, but which actually betrays our deep unhappiness and not understanding why all this is necessary.

In this sense, competition leads to developing only personal qualities that will enable us to win the competition, achieve higher academic results and to be selected. In this competition, selfishness is the leader, when all our energy is directed only to ourselves and what is important only to us. Self-satisfaction, arrogance, the pursuit of materialism and consumerism are accompanying qualities and feelings that are the result of competition. Hypocrisy, pandering, jostling to get ahead, bribery, corruption, unethical and immoral tactics can ensure that we gain the results that we want, but not in a sincere way.

This is what school mainly teaches them; how to fit into society. Hence the dramas of teenagers at school, because their natural aspirations and instincts push them towards something else entirely. They do not want to fit in, they want to be out, and they want to stand out. This is precisely why the competitive spirit is a double-edged sword. It offers opportunities to become part of the social and consumer, but it does not offer opportunities for spiritual growth. In fact, the competition and pragmatism that underlies the pursuit of high results is an obstacle to spiritual growth, which begins when you learn how to overcome the materialism. It is also a willingness to see what lies behind it, even when you are willing to sacrifice the material.

Adolescents are not yet ready for this, as they do not know how to combine both the pragmatism of society and the denial of the energy fusion that comes with it. Pragmatism is the exact opposite of the qualities that teenagers admire and aspire to as they grow up. They are idealists who strive for justice and adventure, they are free in spirit and intent on breaking the status quo, they are rebels who have come to destroy to build something their own and different. They are adaptable and are forced to undergo several transformations in a personal plan. Adolescents then become open to the new and are ready to experiment. They are so close to the state of inner freedom that the only thing that prevents them from practicing it in harmony and peace is the fact that they constantly have to fight for this inner freedom. For them to have their own personal space, a little place inside themselves where they can take off the mask of obedient children and just be themselves, without the expectations that adults have of them. There is a natural human right, which teenagers actually have to fight for. These battles constantly accompany their lives, and as adults with a large magnifying glass constantly monitoring what is happening. Yes, adults have their reasons and fears for controlling their children. There is a huge contradiction amongst adolescents. On the one hand, there are the expectations of adults and the qualities that they should display in front of them, which arise from the pragmatic goals that adults have already set. On the contrary, the adolescent nature which resists pragmatism and frameworks, and which desperately fights for its right to be what it senses and feels with its heart.

Adolescents need adults around them who understand this contradiction and who do not want to kill idealistic and freedom-loving impulses, but, on the contrary, want to nurture them. If they succeed in doing that, they will succeed in raising people who are not only thinking, but also feeling, compassionate and merciful. People who are not content to just stay in their little social dream trap, but one who figures out ways to improve the lives of others, driven by their idealism and free spirit.

We need more idealists and humanists. People who are not only concerned about their salary, but who use their energy and influence to create. Creative energy is the energy of life, and it never stays locked in one form for long, as it always finds a way to continue its life in a new form. Adolescents deserve to be surrounded by spiritually elevated adults who understand and accept them with all the contradictions of their age. Meditation practices are an ideal tool and bridge through which adults and adolescents can walk together toward mutual spiritual growth and communication.

CHILDREN - OUR GUESTS FROM THE FUTURE

Adults are from the past, teenagers are from the future. We carry with us the methods we were raised with, and they smash them to pieces because they no longer work for them. What choice do we have? To change and to make up the distance between adults and children. Yesterday belongs to us, tomorrow belongs to them, but we meet on the stage of today, and this short period of time should be filled with joy and mutual pleasure in communication, which will stimulate both sides to develop.

Yesterday brings with it the memories, the disappointments, the melancholy of something from the past, irreversible, the bitter experience or the joy of luck, it brings love and separation, pain, balance, realism, and pragmatism, to name a few.

Tomorrow is full of beautiful sunrises, a questing and adventurous spirit, dreams, and a hope that tomorrow will somehow avoid the mistakes of yesterday by itself. It is a faith in ideals, optimism that people are better than evil, and second chances should be given. Illusions that God's only concern is to protect us and only us, and therefore frivolity and carelessness about tomorrow often accompany sunrises.

What does today offer, in whose arena the adult meets the adolescent? A combination of both, making communication impossible at times. How do you convince someone to be careful about tomorrow? Is it because people can hurt them? Is it because we want to protect children from betrayal and any other negativity? In their desire to protect adolescents from their negative experiences, go so far as to put them under a glass cover to protect them from anything, just to keep them from getting hurt. However, how do you get to know life and love if you only observe them from your cell? It is not possible to live someone else's life, let alone for them. On today's stage, the adult must be more of a diplomat than the greatest diplomats in the history of diplomacy. They must release the bird that loves to learn only to fly, accepting that the price will be many falls and injuries. This is the only way to develop endurance and courage, to become resistant to storms. The dove teaches its young to fly, helps it with its wings, but after it learns to fly, the dove does not constantly chase it to correct it and tell it how to fly. Nature is wise because it does not doubt, but simply follows the processes of its cyclicity laid down by cosmic intelligence. A person often consciously interferes with these processes. An independent personality can only be built if it is allowed to have independent actions.

I hope someone has not yet been left with the wrong conclusion that we are offering some kind of super liberal and free philosophy in terms of upbringing, a kind of total freedom for teenagers. This is so far from the intention of this book to exist. Its main goal was to familiarize ourselves with the specifics of the main processes that adolescents go through and to look for their place in the general picture of everything changing around us. Only then will we get to know them better and understand what is happening to them and how it affects them mentally and emotionally. When we know them better, we will also find the way to our own change, to find dignified methods and behaviour with which to communicate with each other. Interactions between us should not be based on authoritarian-command methods, but on humane ones. This is the only way to raise future humanists, not authoritarian people. Both at school and at home, if teenagers do not conform to acceptable behaviour norms, do not follow the rules, and do not show good manners, it is the job of the adults around them to set a good example and teach them what the rules are for in society and what is the point of them. Here it is important how this is done, with authoritarian command or humane approach, respecting them as individuals with rights. By shouting or by respecting their honour and dignity? If someone does not want to do something, then no one can make them. You cannot force anyone to do anything. Violence has its consequences, and they are usually mirrored violence. In this sense, it is true that violence begets violence. Instead of insisting and nervously stamping your foot and becoming ridiculous in their eyes, it is better to choose diplomacy. Diplomacy is evasiveness in dealing with other people, avoiding direct confrontations to achieve one's own goals. Diplomacy is the art of achieving the impossible. In this sense, it is a creative skill that combines manipulation and the ability to read psychological profiles.

Therefore, in the course of any negotiations or other contacts, the diplomat must be able to give way to what is not important for their country, protecting the essential. To do this, a true diplomat must have an understanding of what is paramount to their country and the country with which they are negotiating with. This, in turn, will require a different, more in-depth level of knowledge than the excellent command of a foreign language. The ability to win over the interlocutor or correctly draw up an official document. It requires an ability to immerse yourself not only in the official information about the country, but also in its history and customs, its contemporary realities, and political orientations. That is why one of the most important qualities of a diplomat is the ability to work with people and information. You are required to be interesting, intelligent, and outgoing. Invisible victories are part of the backroom negotiations of diplomats that help to get out of deep crises. Tolerance and a sense of measure and tact are the indispensable qualities of the diplomats. If the sense of measure is lacking, it can blow up the situation and destroy the chance of peace talks. The sense of measure is built as a result of observations and judgment of the participants in the dialogue. It is the intuition and gut feeling of knowing when to stop so you do not screw it up. Other important qualities of the diplomat are qualities such as loyalty, honesty, intelligence, broad and deep knowledge in various fields, attentiveness, calmness, restraint, modesty, courage, politeness, diligence, flexibility, caution, observant mind, sociability, personal charm, and charisma.

Diplomacy is what prevents wars. War begins when diplomacy fails in negotiations. Therefore, in a conflict situation, step back, listen to their opinion, talk, discuss, and respect their choice. Teenagers love to have an opinion about everything and share it. Even if you do not like it, the Earth will not stop spinning just because you have different opinions and insist on different things. Be cunning and manipulative, but in a positive way. Appreciate them for being proactive and having their own opinion, this is a happy fact. Negotiate and compromise. You should do your best to keep your relationship with them on a high intelligent level, which is the most important thing, and not turn them against you. Opinions come and go, but the feeling of rejection from close adults and even from teachers accumulates over time and turns into an unwillingness to share with you because you will reject and criticise them anyway. Keep the level up. The teenager should feel after their conversation with you significant and respected, smiling and admired. It is your job to instil that sense of self-respect in them. Let them take the stage of their lives as the main character. After all, everything is temporary, and they are now learning the rules and initiative.

In school, you do not have to fight to death either. If the teenager does not want to follow the rules in the school, that is why there are internal rules and procedures that need to be activated. If he does not follow the rules because they do not understand them, then explain their meaning to them. But in general, that is the point of belonging to a society, you accept the rules as they are. If you cannot change them, you just follow them, it makes everyday communication and activities easier.

There are no knobs and buttons that we press, and we will get the desired behaviour and attitude in adolescents. They are not robots. Relationships are a complex process in which both parties must want something beautiful to happen. In this sense, no adult guide that gives advice on quick results works. You must know your children and students, and you must have constant communication built on mutual liking and respect. You must enjoy talking, sharing, laughing together, learning different new things, growing intellectually and spiritually together. This also applies to teachers. A teacher who thinks that they have nothing to learn from a student, does not understand the meaning of their own profession.

Teenagers are space aliens who have come to remind us of our own nature and the free, and the independent nature of the ever-changing cosmos. They are the spokesmen on behalf of cosmic processes that we must delicately and wisely guide in the direction of painless adaptation to social structures and norms of behaviour.

Adults often make various naïve appeals about the importance of keeping the child within us, or which becomes a beautiful sad metaphor for something irretrievably gone. What is usually meant is freedom from social constraints, the ability to spontaneously respond to what is happening around us and no matter how judgmental the reactions of other adults may be. The ability to believe and realise all the potential of that tomorrow, in which teenagers so beautifully and romantically believe. Adults often envy children and adolescents for this spontaneity and impulsiveness in expressing thoughts and feelings. This is because whatever teenagers do, they do it with all their heart and soul. It does not matter if it will be doubt, adventurism, melodramatics, naivety, inexperience or first love. They experience it as you experience something you feel for the first time. Genuinely and with faith, this is their thing. This is why grumbling and criticising adults from the scene of their yesterday are sometimes so annoying to teenagers. They simply speak from the space of their social frameworks, voluntarily losing their naivety, illusions, spontaneity, and impulsiveness.

If adults enable themselves to part with their deeply built habits and compulsive responses that lead to automaticity and inertia in thought and action, then they will be able to see their sunrise again and feel the kisses of the morning breeze. Habits create a comfortable routine, but habits can also kill. They slowly but surely put us in a framework that becomes similar to our identity. An identity prison in which the freedom to change is completely absent. Often it is a very comfortable frame, it even happens to be gilded, from which it weighs more, because the metal is firmly glued to the frame. It is hung on the wall of your life, and you hang it as an example of social success, obedience, and self-sacrifice.

Teenagers know how to break the boundaries and fly free. Free and different, full of dreams. Adolescents are magical space messengers, and it is imperative that we establish a positive foundation of trust, to help assist their transition from child into a teenager, utilising pedagogical and spiritual conversations along the way.

VISIT MY BLOG

To visit my blog, you can scan this code. You can use a QR scanner app on your phone, or some camera apps.

Alternatively, you can see more about me on my blog by clicking on:

https://phdelenalyubenova.blogspot.com/

Printed in Great Britain
by Amazon